MEANING AND UNDERSTANDING

Foundations of Contemporary Interpretation
Moisés Silva, Series Editor
Volume 2

MEANING AND UNDERSTANDING

The Philosophical Framework for Biblical Interpretation

Royce Gordon Gruenler

ZondervanPublishingHouse
Academic and Professional Books
Grand Rapids, Michigan
A Division of HarperCollins*Publishers*

Requests for information should be addressed to:
Zondervan Publishing House
Academic and Professional Books
1415 Lake Drive S.E.
Grand Rapids, Michigan 49506

Library of Congress Cataloging in Publication Data

Gruenler, Royce Gordon.
Meaning and understanding : the philosophical framework for Biblical interpretation / Royce Gordon Gruenler.
p. cm. – (Foundations of contemporary interpretation : v. 2)
Includes bibliographical references.
ISBN 0-310-40931-4 :
1. Bible–Hermeneutics. 2. Meaning (Philosophy) I. Title. II. Series.
BS476.G78 1991 89-28700
220.6'01–dc20 CIP

Edited by Gerard Terpstra and Leonard G. Goss
Cover Design by Art Jacobs

Printed in the United States of America

91 92 93 94 95 / CH / 10 9 8 7 6 5 4 3 2 1

In Grateful Memory of Faithful Teachers

Fred Carl Kuehner
Robert K. Rudolph
Theophilus J. Herter

CONTENTS

EDITOR'S PREFACE

The present work, volume 2 of *Foundations of Contemporary Interpretation*, serves a twofold purpose. In the first place, it functions as a bridge between volume 1, which was primarily historical in character, and the other books in the series. The first volume could deal only superficially with the modern period. In contrast, Professor Gruenler is able to focus, with some detail, on those philosophical developments of the last two centuries that most directly affect biblical interpretation.

In the second place, however, the author moves beyond historical description to critique the basic assumptions of contemporary theological scholarship. By doing so, he seeks to provide a coherent philosophical platform on which responsible exegesis may rest. Biblical interpreters, not infrequently, go about their work as though they were immune to the non-Christian, and even anti-Christian, bias that characterizes modern Western thought. A careful reading of this book should quickly dispel that illusion.

The author is uniquely qualified to deal with these concerns. As a highly respected New Testament scholar, he is fully aware of the technical problems faced by biblical exegesis. Earlier in his career, however—indeed, prior to his commitment to the evangelical faith—he was a teacher of philosophy and religion, and in that capacity he had opportunity to reflect on the broad, basic questions posed by the great thinkers of civilization. If he writes aggressively and with conviction, the reason is not to be sought in the kind of knee-jerk overreaction typical of some Christian groups, but rather in his first-hand acquaintance with two opposing principles of thought.

Young students of the Bible may be inclined to set aside

philosophical discussion as abstract or theoretical or irrelevant. They only do so at their peril. The demands of contemporary society call for biblical interpreters willing to confront the tough questions head-on. Professor Gruenler will prove a wise guide in that task.

Moisés Silva

INTRODUCTION

God's common grace in creation affords a vast fund of knowledge that Christians as well as non-Christians may draw on. This is the assumption of the Foundations of Contemporary Interpretation series and of this particular volume on the philosophical underpinnings of biblical interpretation. The book concludes realistically, however, that in spite of common data and often common methodology, there remains a basic and unresolved conflict between evangelical and nonevangelical scholars. While the latter generally attempt to separate faith and objective historical reality into compartments, evangelicals are strongly committed to historical questions in context of the authority and reliability of Scripture.

The underlying principles of biblical hermeneutics accordingly are bound up with fundamental epistemological questions of knowing. Evangelicals are committed to the belief that the Holy Spirit gives the believer a new understanding to acknowledge and enjoy God and what he has made and that the Spirit's internal testimony works in accord with his general revelation in the created world. On the one hand, Scripture implies that knowledge of God and of the world comes "naturally" by way of God's common grace in creation, as he sustains and interprets whatever he brings into being and places knowledge of himself and the world in the human mind. Hence his self-disclosures in Scripture, in the world, and in human experience are interrelated. Classical biblical passages that espouse this view are Psalm 19:1–6 and Romans 1:19–20. On the other hand, most philosophies do not reckon with scriptural teaching about the heredity of sin, which has infected the natural order and the reliability of the mind to discover ultimate truth (Rom. 1:18,

21–25). According to the Scriptures, a radical turnabout of one's thought and life must precede a valid understanding of God, the world, and the self (John 3:3, 5; 2 Cor. 5:17; 1 Peter 1:23). Although basic knowledge of God and creation lies deep within human beings by way of God's common grace (Rom. 1:19–20), it is suppressed by rebellion against God: "Since they did not think it worthwhile to retain the knowledge of God, he gave them over to a depraved mind, to do what ought not to be done" (Rom. 1:28). In the unnatural state of rebellion against God, one knows the ultimate reality of things, yet does not know to the point of obedience to God, which comes through the transformation of thought and behavior.

Philosophical exploration is therefore a valuable tool of the human mind. But it is unreliable unless it is used judiciously according to some higher principle of discrimination brought about through the work of regeneration by the Holy Spirit. The Christian scholar must always test the spirits (1 Cor. 12:10; 1 John 4:1) in light of the higher norm of Scripture. Much may be learned from philosophical methods and insights if these are used with discernment, and important corrections from a scriptural perspective can often bring philosophical beliefs and systems to their proper fulfillment. It is important to bear in mind, however, that Scripture teaches a definite hierarchy of authority by which God's Word takes precedence over his revelation in nature and self, requiring a rebirthing of the heart and mind. Two biblical examples will suffice, one from Jesus, the other from Paul.

When Jesus came into Galilee at the beginning of his ministry, his proclamation (*kerygma*) embraced three propositions (Mark 1:14–15): (1) The messianic time foretold by the prophets of old has been fulfilled; (2) the people were subject to the reign of God (inaugurated in Jesus' own person); (3) therefore, they were to repent and believe the Good News. In this capsule summary of his message Jesus signified the meaning of the present time by focusing on himself Old Testament prophecies about the Messiah and the reign of God, thereby challenging his hearers to a new understanding of their familiar faith. He offered them an interpretation of Scripture that would transform their entire outlook on the world and redeem their lives eternally. But they had to believe if they were to understand. That is why, having made two parallel statements in respect to the nature of the momentous "kairotic" time he was inaugurating (points 1 and 2), he exhorted his hearers to experience a transformation of their thought about him, themselves, and the world: "Repent [*metanoeite*] and believe [*pisteuete*] the good news!" (point 3).

Similarly, Paul exhorts his readers (Rom. 12:2) not to conform their lives to the schematic of this fallen age. The Christian metamorphosis which comes through conversion to Christ may accordingly be termed a *metanoetic* transformation of thought (from *meta*, "change," and *nous*, "mind") because it focuses on the mind's new openness to God's objective Word and the reorientation of patterns of thought and behavior.

These exhortations of Jesus and Paul to decisive faith and change of basic orientation sum up the important biblical teaching that persons are essentially defined by the way they conceive of God and act in private and in public (the propositional and performative factors, respectively). According to the Scriptures, human beings are created in the image of God and they are to think his thoughts after him. Hence the human mind contains a spectrum of images by which one chooses either to order speech in action faithfully in accordance with God's revelations of truth in the human self, creation, and Scripture or unfaithfully in conformity to one's fallen and autonomous interpretations of reality. Hermeneutics in the broadest sense is concerned with these interpretations of the world that a person asserts to be true and by which one's life is ordered, for better or for worse. Since this book deals with a wide range of philosophical perspectives, the term "hermeneutics" will sometimes be used in this larger epistemological sense. In the series as a whole, however, as well as in this book, it bears special reference to the foundational principles that help us understand the nature and function of biblical interpretation. The sections in our study that deal with philosophical aids to specific exegetical texts or problems will be found in chapters 4 and 7, although each chapter addresses larger exegetical questions.

Meaning and understanding accordingly reside in each person's mind or "heart," for it is there that the objective messages from the real God and his real world collide with the distorted messages from the demonic kingdom and where choices are made and a life is either won or lost. The question of hermeneutical viewpoint is thus the key issue in life and is not to be thought of solely as the science that informs the interpretation and application of Scripture, although that is one of its major functions for the biblical interpreter. The scope of hermeneutics is all-embracing and serves to disclose the inner patterns of meaning and intention that identify each human being and determine the presuppositions one brings to the interpretation of Scripture.

Standing in the prophetic tradition of Jeremiah 29:13—"You will seek me and find me when you seek me with all your heart"—Jesus presents his critics with the challenge that nothing in the outer world makes a person unclean; it is inner thoughts and intentions which shape one's view of the world: "Listen to me, everyone, and understand this. Nothing outside a man can make him 'unclean'" (Mark 7:14–15; cf. Matt. 5:20, the focus of the Sermon on the Mount, [Matt. 5–7]). Jesus persistently drives inward to personal thought and integrity, to the "heart," where one's controlling view of the world resides and expresses itself in bodily speech and acts. In the fallen world to which he came Jesus consistently assaulted hypocrisy, a deceptive form of hermeneutics that, then as now, seeks to misuse speech and action to veil a different intent, causing the eventual disintegration of self, speech, and society. In his own person Jesus exemplified purity and integrity of intention and behavior, bearing witness to the ultimate hermeneutical principle that characterizes the Triune Family.[1]

In the divine Trinity meaning and understanding are shared on the highest level by Father, Son, and Holy Spirit in dynamic and inexhaustible communion and unity.[2] This mean-

---

[1]See Royce Gordon Gruenler, *The Trinity in the Gospel of John: A Thematic Commentary on the Fourth Gospel* (Grand Rapids: Baker, 1986).

[2]See Royce Gordon Gruenler, *The Inexhaustible God: Biblical Faith and the Challenge of Process Theism* (Grand Rapids: Baker, 1983).

ing is imprinted on creation by the divine signature but is suppressed by human rebellion against God and his interpretation of reality. Accordingly, as incarnate Son of God, Son of Man, and Suffering Servant, Jesus redemptively transposes the grid of divine meaning to the fallen level by laying down his life of perfection on the cross and satisfying all righteousness, rising from death with the power of new life and understanding. Through the Holy Spirit he brings into being a new community that shares his meaning and understanding as servants to a lost world. But always the new hermeneutics the Spirit brings assumes the basic validity of God's general revelation in the world and the self. In their common redemptive ministry, Father, Son, and Spirit superimpose special revelation upon the meaning already present in creation through divine creative activity in the initial and continual framing of the world. The special revelation of Scripture is always given in respect to the structures of meaning and language already impressed on creation. Hence an examination of philosophical explorations of the world and the self may prove to be profitable if pursued with the gift of discerning the spirits (1 Cor. 12:10).

This study in comparative hermeneutics from the perspective of philosophical analysis is therefore deeply informed by the meaning and significance of Scripture. A major focus of the study is the Copernican revolution in hermeneutical thought inaugurated by Immanuel Kant in the closing quarter of the eighteenth century. Kant drew together the two strains of rationalism and empiricism inherited from his predecessors, themselves heirs of the Renaissance, and concentrated them into a new interpretive synthesis. He powerfully influenced Enlightenment and post-Enlightenment criticism far into the nineteenth and twentieth centuries. An understanding of the Kantian system, with its exaltation of the human mind as the source of meaning and understanding, provides a model of modern interpretation and its effects on the significance of Scripture and biblical exegesis.

It is my hope that this book will serve as an aid and encouragement to further study by which the reader may analyze more maturely modern philosophical viewpoints that have had enormous impact on the interpretation of the Bible. Part 1 will focus on the systems of rationalism, especially idealism, that have characterized European thought since the Kantian revolution in epistemology. At the end of the section, some helpful models for biblical exegesis will be drawn from one of the representatives of Continental thought, Gabriel Marcel. Part 2 will concentrate on Anglo-American schools of empiricism and realism and their suggestions for fresh insights into biblical hermeneutics. While in the past, idealism has been far more pervasive in biblical studies in Britain and America, as well as on the Continent, there is in the modern period a distinctive strain of realism in certain philosophical schools, particularly in the English-speaking world. This trend holds considerable promise for a fresh hermeneutical outlook that will be conducive to biblical realism. At the close of part 2, practical application will be made of the philosophical method of Michael Polanyi—a method that offers numerous aids to the biblical interpreter.

If the present study makes a contribution to the ongoing hermeneutical discussion, it will be largely along the lines of a philosophical realism that acknowledges God's empirical self-disclosure in his Word, in nature, and in human experience. The Bible, I will argue, is to be seen as God's objective revelation of the way things are to be interpreted under his lordship. It is my conviction that hermeneutics is first of all the enterprise of God, who by common grace has already interpreted the world and the human self in his creation. He has interpreted us and our world afresh through the special redemptive grace of Jesus Christ, attested by Holy Scripture through inspiration of the Holy Spirit. The ideas of the mind are crucial, and in this respect idealism has validity in the search for meaning. Yet in the biblical tradition truth-bearing ideas are always underwritten by the reality of God and the objectivity of his revelation in Scripture, world, and self. The only guarantee against the dualism and ultimately subjective idealism that has been the legacy of Kantian criticism is God and his objective disclosure of "the nature of the case" in his holy and inspired Word. God's Word brings to light his already present revelation in the world and in the mind. This is of foundational importance as we attempt to articulate more clearly the philosophical principles of biblical interpretation in our quest for ultimate meaning and significance.

A futher word on methodology will be helpful to the reader. Normally an analysis will proceed on three levels: first, an accurate presentation of the point of view under consideration; second, an attempt to describe the similarities between that point of view and biblical faith in view of general revelation, highlighting any helpful insights that might aid the task of biblical interpretation; third, a critique of the viewpoint from the perspective of special revelation in Scripture. Limitations of space did not permit analysis on level two of every philosophy considered in this study. Accordingly, major focus is on select cases, with an overall critique of Kantian hermeneutics on level three. Various readers will doubtless find useful aids for biblical meaning and understanding in philosophical schools that call for further exploration.

Part 1

HERMENEUTICS FROM THE PERSPECTIVE OF EUROPEAN IDEALISM

1

UNDERSTANDING THE KANTIAN LEGACY

In order to appreciate the tremendous impact of philosophical ideas on biblical hermeneutics in the last two centuries, it is important to understand the thought of the most influential philosophical figure in modern Western philosophy, Immanuel Kant (1724–1804). Kant stands at the apex of the Renaissance-Enlightenment movement, and apart from him the unfolding of hermeneutical programs in our contemporary era cannot be fully understood or appreciated. The date 1781 is as notable in the history of ideas as in the shaping of the American Republic. In that year Kant published his *Critique of Pure Reason (Kritik der reinen Vernunft)*, a book that Moses Mendelssohn, grandfather of the composer, described as the "all-smasher."[1] Within critical circles it eventually succeeded in smashing the dominant influence of traditional philosophy, theology, hermeneutics, and biblical interpretation that had held sway for centuries. Kant's study marks not only the high point of the Enlightenment but the virtual end of the old order. Today hardly a college, university, or theological seminary (a few conservative ones excepted) remain uninfluenced in some substantial way by the Kantian hermeneutical revolution. Its influence reaches outward pervasively to other fields of thought and to general culture itself.

---

[1]Quoted in Walter Kaufmann, *Philosophic Classics: Bacon to Kant* (Englewood Cliffs, N.J.: Prentice-Hall, 1961), 416.

Kant's Copernican revolution in the realm of critical thought and hermeneutics replaced the authority of Scripture with the autonomy of the human mind, making experience and reason the focus of authority in the quest for understanding the meaning of the world and human existence. In formulating his hermeneutics Kant dealt seriously with the thought of his philosophical predecessors from two streams of thought: Continental rationalism, with its emphasis on logic and reason, and British empiricism, with its analysis of experience. Both were children of the Renaissance and, unlike the Protestant Reformers, shifted the focus of authority from the study of God and Scripture to the study of man and the world. One can see this paradigm shift already taking place in sixteenth-century literature as Shakespeare moved the vertical drama from inside the cathedral to the horizontal drama outside in the theatre of humanity. Art, too, became more fascinated with human form and landscapes and with classical mythology and contemporary subjects than with biblical or heavenly themes. Science began its rise to eventual prominence in Western thought by concentrating on the physical world and human ability to fathom and control its structures of power. Accordingly, where biblical and Reformation thought give God primary focus and view humanity as subsidiary, the children of the Renaissance and the Enlightenment have accorded humanity primary authority and made God subsidiary. Kant inherits this legacy.

KANT'S PREDECESSORS

Kant held that knowledge is attainable without recourse to any special or supernatural revelation. To demonstrate how he constructs his imaginative and complex philosophical method, we will briefly consider three hermeneuticians from each of the two principal schools mentioned above who contributed to his final hermeneutical synthesis. Those representing Continental rationalism are Descartes, Spinoza, and Leibniz. Those representing British empiricism are Locke, Berkeley, and Hume. With the basic arguments of these six men in view we will better understand Kant's innovative and wide-reaching hermeneutical system, for it drew on the impetus of their thought. Kant's hermeneutics profoundly influenced nineteenth- and twentieth-century thought.

The Continental Rationalists: Descartes, Spinoza, Leibniz

The three representative philosophers representing Continental rationalists were brilliant and imaginative (though not always consistent) logicians who attempted to derive truth deductively from the rational structure of the mind on the pattern of mathematics and analytical geometry. All were theists but in various ways unorthodox. Descartes and Leibniz were of Christian persuasion but interpreted God more as a necessary part of their logical systems than as the self-revealing Deity of Scripture. Spinoza, Jewish by birth, repudiated biblical faith and argued for a closed system of impersonal pantheism in which everything is a part of God. Although their logical systems differ, they all agree that human reason is sufficient to deduce all necessary truth and that one can even prove the existence of God by rational argument without recourse to Scripture.

René Descartes (1596–1650). Ironically, belief in God combined with radical doubt initially characterizes Descartes' search for absolutely certain knowledge. Everything in the realm of the senses and of time and space (including history) I can doubt, he argues, but one thing I cannot doubt, and that is the fact that I doubt (*dubito*); and since I think, therefore I am (*cogito ergo sum*). This is pure and clear logic, he reasons, free of the deceptions of the senses.[2] Although he is a convinced theist, Descartes does not appeal to Scripture as the source of true and certain knowledge about the world and the self and God, for sure knowledge comes by the logical reasoning of the mind alone. Since it is the authoritative *I* which reasons in its search for truth, there is a radical reduction of authority to the

[2]René Descartes, *Descartes: Philosophical Writings*, trans. and eds. Elizabeth Anscombe and P. T. Geach (London: Thomas Nelson, 1964), 32, 74.

reasoning self, for all else is in doubt in the reduction. Once the rational thinking self is established as the original given of authority, the philosopher can work outward from the rational mind to conceive of the physical world entirely in logical terms as a mathematical extension in space and time, subject to logically deducible laws.[3]

One can even reason that ultimately and logically there must be a God: (1) one can imagine a being who possesses all attributes, therefore he must exist since existence is a necessary attribute; (2) God is logically necessary to save one from deception and to guarantee the reality of a mechanical world, although (3) it is not necessary for God to have created a world, since he freely chose to create it.[4] This last argument poses a further problem about Descartes' hermeneutics, for he believes that the real self lies in the soul and, like God, is free. In the realm of the body and physical nature there is no freedom, for all creatures are machines in space where everything is logically related and predictable by the mathematics of physics—the geometry of space. In Descartes' mind the material world is mechanistic, a view that seems to reflect the discoveries of the new world of science emerging in his day. Yet he wants somehow to hold on to the freedom of the self and does so by identifying the self with the soul that is unextended in space and time and transcends the mechanism of the body and of nature.[5]

Hence there arises a radical dualism of two basic substances in the world, the one mechanical and confined to space, the other free and transcending space. The perplexing question is how the transcendent freedom of the ego relates to the behaviorally conditioned mechanism of the body. The best Descartes can do is to locate the soul in the pineal gland at a point without extension through which the animal spirits of the body course and are influenced by the force of the soul.[6] It is not a solution that is accepted today. Yet Descartes' dualism remains with us in remarkably influential patterns. This appears

---

[3]Ibid., 34–35.

[4]Ibid., 33–37, 76–91.

[5]Ibid., 66–75, 109–24, 199–221.

[6]Ibid., 241–56.

in modern liberal and neoorthodox theologies and biblical methodologies, in which biblical history lies in the realm of behavioral cause-and-effect while freedom lies in the realm of ineffable encounter with God. Cartesian dualism is also present in nontheistic philosophies such as the existentialism of Jean-Paul Sartre who argues for the transcendent freedom of the ego ("for myself," *pour moi*) over against mechanical nature (being "in itself," *en soi*), which threatens to devour the free and processing self.[7]

Descartes has been called the father of modern philosophy, and in many respects that is true in spite of his indebtedness to classical philosophy, medieval scholasticism, and Catholic Christianity. His principal legacy to his successors, to Kant, and to the modern world is his dualistic conception of reality as two opposing poles—the primary pole of the free and autonomous thinking self and the pole of deterministic nature. In a sense he may be credited with a *tour de force* in turning classical philosophical dualism upside down. Plato and his successors saw the dialectical tension between form and matter and gave pride of place to form and continuity, in contrast to the threatening world of matter with its illogic and discontinuity. Descartes and his modern progeny have given primacy to the freedom pole of the ego (the principle of indeterminacy and discontinuity), in contrast to the threatening world of matter, the pole of scientific and technocratic rationalism (the principle of behavioral determinism and continuity). Descartes' influence on Kant was substantial, as we shall see. While Descartes was a devout Catholic (no one can read him without sensing his deep religious convictions), his God is not the God of Abraham, Isaac, and Jacob, or of grace and salvation from sin, for sin is not a philosophical concept and plays no role in his thought.

Baruch Spinoza (1632–1677). Spinoza was a Dutch philosopher whose orthodox Jewish lineage descended from ancestors who had fled the Inquisition in Spain and Portugal, but he relinquished his orthodoxy and was excommunicated by

[7]See Jean-Paul Sartre, *The Transcendence of the Ego* (New York, 1937); idem, *Being and Nothingness* (New York, 1956).

the Jewish community in 1656. With Descartes, he agreed that the rational mind is the seat of authority and that reason and logic are capable of accurately describing reality. But he attempted to correct Descartes' mind/body dualism by uniting all existence with the infinite substance of God, thus conceiving of a pantheistic monism in which God is nature and nature is God.[8] In this system space, time, matter, and all existence are manifestations of divine substance; human thought, with everything else, is an aspect or mode of impersonal infinite divinity in which all is logically determined and chance is impossible. In Spinoza's radical rationalism this actual world could not be otherwise, for God makes no choices from other possibilities. This world is perfect, necessary, and complete because God is perfect, necessary, and complete.[9]

One can see how far Spinoza has moved away from the God of the Bible and the extent to which his hermeneutics is controlled, not by Scripture, but by the autonomy of the rational mind.[10] Questions arise as to the rationality of the system, however, for by investing God with an infinite number of attributes, including space and materiality, he makes the divine substance everything generally and nothing specifically. For Spinoza, God is not the infinite and personal Being who transcends the individual modes of human persons.

The net effect of Spinoza's monism is both a radical deconstruction of the transcendent sovereign God of Scripture, who calls nature into being and sustains it by the word of his power, and the elevation of man and all else to the level of divinity in a closed pantheistic system in which autonomous human reason is enthroned as authoritative. Descartes' free-ranging transcendent ego is sacrificed to the logical system. For Spinoza, human consciousness of freedom is merely uncon-

---

[8]See *The Chief Works of Benedict de Spinoza*, trans. and ed. R. H. M. Lewis (New York: Dover Publications, 1951), vol. 1, chaps. 1–15.

[9]Ibid., vol. 2, Proposition XXXVI.

[10]Philosophy (or Reason) and Scripture are to be kept in separate compartments. See ibid., 1:190–98. For Spinoza's critical assessment of Scripture, see ibid., 13–180. See also A. Wolf, trans. and ed., *Spinoza's Short Treatise on God, Man, and His Well-Being* (New York: Russell & Russell, 1963).

sciousness of the factors that cause us to behave as we do. To be truly free, he argues, is to deduce our freedom from God, who exists solely by the necessity of his own nature. It is to accept the logical necessity of reality, coming to know things as they really are and realizing that nothing is ultimately good or bad, just or unjust, including death itself. Like the Hindu and the Buddhist, one must not desire to attach oneself to things that have only relative value but rest in knowledge of the inevitability of reality and conceive of everything under the form of eternal logic.

Spinoza pays a higher price than the Hindu pantheist, however, for the latter has a goal of deliverance from the world (however cyclical), whereas in Spinoza's divine world one has no particular place to go, since his world is already perfect and fully actual. There is no immortal soul, as in Plato, and no resurrection from the dead, as in Christianity. There is only eternal logic, which has no vital relation to time. Kant will accept Spinoza's insistence on the right of the rational mind to define reality, but he will take the world of time, space, and experience more seriously and attempt to bring the two realms into dialectical relationship. Others like Goethe, Lessing, Herder, Fichte, Schelling, and Hegel will accord Spinoza's pantheistic determinism and identification of God and nature a prominent role in the hermeneutics of the eighteenth and nineteenth centuries.

Gottfried Leibniz (1646–1716). Like Descartes and Spinoza, Leibniz engaged in the scientific thought of his time and viewed reality largely from the perspective of reason, deductive logic, and mathematics (he developed calculus independently of Newton's earlier work). He disagreed, however, with Descartes' dualistic division of reality into unextended thinking souls and extended unthinking bodies.[11] He also disagreed with Spinoza's reduction of thought and extension to attributes of a single pantheistic substance.[12] His view was that the world is

[11]See Philip P. Wiener, ed., *Leibniz: Selections* (New York: Scribner, 1951), 90–91.

[12]Ibid., 485–97.

composed of simple and unified substances called monads. Monads have neither size nor shape but are all qualitatively different and therefore afford maximum beauty in this best of all possible worlds by their unity in diversity.[13] Leibniz describes these monads as an infinite group of souls that are subject to continuous change within themselves but cannot interact with each other because they are windowless (since substance cannot interact). However, each reflects in itself the universe, and all work together by the preestablished harmony of God as each monad plays the particular score God as written for it.

Leibniz asserts that these monads all perceive on a graded scale of intensity. Hence the world is composed of perceiving souls who exhibit a vital principle or force of life, God being the supreme monad who shapes the world. Since material and mechanical things neither exhibit this life force nor perceive anything, materialism is, for Leibniz, logically impossible. What, then, of matter and body? Since matter is extended in space, it cannot be substance, for only the unextended soul or monad has substance and perceives and exhibits life force. Matter, or body, is therefore a multitude or concentration of monads arranged in a hierarchy of intensity of perception. In the human body there is one dominant monad (the soul) and many lower monads that are held together by God's preestablished harmony, by which he affords freedom of will while still shaping the world as the best of all possible worlds. (Later, in the twentieth century, the process philosopher Charles Hartshorne adapted the theory of dominant and graded monads in his organismic system).[14]

While sympathetic to Christianity, Leibniz makes no exegetical use of Scripture to inform his view of God, persons, and the world, but in the spirit of the age he accords to reason the authority to deduce the nature of reality from the human mind. But as with Descartes and Spinoza, the autonomous

[13]Ibid., 533–52.

[14]See the discussion of Hartshorne, Whitehead, and process theism, below, pp. 135–39 and 162–67.

rational mind has brought Leibniz the rationalist to an irrational set of opposites or antinomies. Not only has he failed to show how the mind can logically interact with the body, but he also makes it impossible for minds to interact with other minds and bodies. Yet as a scientist he sees these interactions taking place constantly before his eyes. Only by appeal to the preestablished harmony of God as composer and conductor can the disparate units play together as an orchestra; and for that reason it is the best possible orchestra. For all his ingenious insights, however, it is clear that Leibniz really gives pride of place to the authority of the human mind, not to the revelation of God in Scripture. He also passed along to Kant and his successors a dialectical tension between the pole of freedom located in the ego and the pole of mechanical cause and effect located in nature.

The British Empiricists: John Locke, George Berkeley, and David Hume

In contrast to the Continental rationalists for whom the logical realm of the mind is uppermost, the early British philosophers concentrate on experience derived from sense perception. The self is no less authoritative in the quest to understand the meaning of reality; simply, the hermeneutical focus has shifted from the logical self to the sensory self. Under attack are the notions of innate ideas and *a priori* truths, and in the foreground is the practical world of the senses. Even though we allow for the later interaction of rationalism and empiricism in the dialectical synthesis of Kant and his successors, it is nevertheless true even today that British (and to a large extent American) philosophy, theology, and hermeneutical method remain strongly practical and empirical when compared to the more cerebral idealism characteristic of Continental hermeneutics. Because of the widely influential work of Locke, Berkeley, and Hume, the eighteenth century may be called the century of empirical hermeneutics, whereas the seventeenth century was more the century of rationalist hermeneutics. The nineteenth and twentieth centuries will be characterized by a critical synthesis of the two fundamental themes of rationalism and empiricism.

John Locke (1632–1704). The scientific age was blossoming when Locke took up his search for meaning and understanding and published his reflections in *An Essay Concerning Human Understanding.*[15] He observed that ideas commonly held may be derived from ordinary experience, and since no idea is ever held by everybody absolutely and universally, there is little evidence for the notion of innate ideas. Hence all knowledge is based on experience alone. The mind is like a blank tablet (*tabula rasa*) that receives sensations from the external world of reality. At its next stage the mind reflects on these sensations by perception, thinking, reasoning, and willing. Locke was a theist, but he did not fashion his hermeneutics around Scripture, God's self-revelation in nature, or the divine image within the self. Instead of starting from the top down with God's interpretation of reality, he began from the bottom up with simple sensations in human experience that lead to perceptions and the higher levels of compounding, abstracting, and relating ideas.[16]

This pattern, which underlies both Lockean and modern theories of meaning and understanding, may be called the hermeneutics of atomicity. It begins with "atomic" sensations on the lowest level and constructs a rational universe from basic experience upward, like a pyramid rising from the unit blocks at the base to a point at the top. The mind, so it is argued, is thus able to construct abstract universals from particular things, such as *stone* from stones and *book* from books. The mind can assume that beneath or within these particulars is something that identifies them as a group, although when Locke considers how things are individuated from one another and possess their own identity he simply wants to say that a particular existence

[15]For an edited version of Locke's text, based on the abridged version of Mary Whiton Calkins and A. S. Pringle-Pattison, see Kaufmann, *Philosophic Classics*, 187–228.

[16]See ibid., 190–99.

in time and space accounts for individual identity: it is because it is what it is.[17]

There are serious problems in Locke's hermeneutical method, even on his own admission. He is unable to account for (1) the cause of particulars, (2) the underlying substance that unites particulars, and (3) the relation of cause and effect in complex groups such as husband, wife, son, and daughter, who together compose a family. Locke admits that we can know very little even of ourselves, let alone the spiritual realm or God (although he wants to affirm that the existence of God is demonstrably certain and that the goodness of God guarantees that simple ideas conform to external objects). But if we cannot know how primary sensations give rise to secondary levels of perception and ideas, or how the mind relates to the body, how can we be sure that our ideas of reality somehow conform to what is really there?—unless God's self-disclosure in Scripture takes precedence over the speculations of the human mind.

As the father of modern empiricism (probably the most widespread philosophy of our day) Locke has opted for a hermeneutical method that locates meaning and understanding primarily in the experiencing self, without recourse to innate ideas or logic or divinely revealed Scripture. As a consequence, he is able to claim certainty for very little. Later Berkeley saw the problem and relied more heavily on ideas and on God as guarantor of the correspondence between ideas and reality, and Hume dismissed God and necessary relationships altogether, opening the way to a radical skepticism that lies just beneath the surface of empiricism.[18]

George Berkeley (1685–1753). Berkeley was influenced by the empiricism of Locke and held that all perception and knowledge are centered in ideas within the mind. For something to be, it must be perceived by a perceiver. We are rescued from human subjectivism and solipsism, however, by the fact that we see through the mind of God. Since everything God has

---

[17]Ibid., 202–28.

[18]For an able criticism of the dualism and skepticism in Locke's methodology, see Michael Polanyi, *Personal Knowledge* (Chicago: University of Chicago Press, 1974), 266, 271.

created is in his mind, the ideas he produces in our minds provide confidence that what we see corresponds to reality. Some years ago the late Roman Catholic biblical scholar Ronald Knox coined a double limerick to illustrate Berkeley's argument (the setting is a tree in the college quadrangle):[19]

> There was a young man who said, "God
> Must think it exceedingly odd
> If he finds that this tree
> Continues to be
> When there's no one about in the Quad."
>
> Dear Sir: Your astonishment's odd:
> *I* am always about in the Quad.
> And that's why the tree
> Will continue to be
> Since observed by, Yours faithfully, God.

Berkeley was committed to the empiricist doctrine that experience is the source of all knowledge, but he set out to correct Locke in two major works, *A New Theory of Vision*, and *Principles of Human Knowledge*.[20] First, he argues that abstract ideas do not come from particular objects that impress themselves on the blank tablet of the mind, as Locke thought. Rather, all one has to do is observe the contents or ideas of one's own mind. Experience for Berkeley lies in the realm of one's ideas about reality; accordingly, it is with the mind's activity that one must begin. Sophisticated ideas like shape, position, motion, and space are complex experiences of one's own mind, not impressions made by external objects on a blank and passive slate called the self. It is the self who knows and perceives. Without the perceiving mind there is no reality, since all ideas are abstract and exist only in the mind. There is no existence of matter independent of perception (thus Berkeley's empirical idealism and his famous dictum, *esse est percipi*, "to be is to be perceived").[21]

As we have noted, there is danger here of solipsism; i.e.,

---

[19]Quoted in Kaufmann, *Philosophic Classics*, 276.

[20]See Alexander Campbell Fraser, *Selections from Berkeley, Annotated* (Freeport, N.Y.: Books for Libraries Press, 1972 [1899].

[21]Ibid., 36–37, 67–68, 82, 96.

other persons and objects exist only insofar as I perceive them, for reality resides in my mind as I contemplate the experience of my ideas. One might ask, Do other persons and things really exist, and how can I know? But as we have also observed, Berkeley anticipates this problem with his argument that God is the highest perceiving mind through whom we perceive. God guarantees the existence of the external world by arousing in us sensations of the created order.[22]

Although Berkeley and Leibniz are the most orthodox Christians of the six philosophers in our group (Descartes and Locke are more nominally inclined to historic Christianity, while Spinoza and Hume are antagonistic to it), it is problematic, but not unexpected, that their insistence on the authority of the self leads to such different hermeneutical points of view. Leibniz, a rationalist, advances a system of logical deduction based on abstract mathematics; Berkeley advances a system of ideas based on inductive experience by way of the senses. Perhaps the two approaches are complementary and need to be fused into a larger synthesis. Kant certainly thought so, especially if God was to function as the "ghost in the machine" to hold these earlier systems together. Kant would not appeal to God in his *Critique of Pure Reason* but to the transcendental ego, relegating God to the personal and practical side of things in his *Critique of Practical Reason.* He had been baptized in the fire of Hume's skepticism, where the presence of God was burned away from the center of analytic thought and left to function, if at all, only in the realm of religious feeling and ethics. To Hume, then, we turn to understand how the empiricist school finally dispensed with God altogether and was left at last to wrestle with the problem of the unity of the human mind itself.

David Hume (1711–1776). Where Berkeley had argued against an independent material world in favor of a world of ideas resident in the perceiving mind (empirical idealism), Hume took the next step and questioned the reality of any substantial soul or mind at all. Hence the well-known saying among students of philosophy, "No matter (Berkeley), never

---

[22]Ibid., 36, 86.

mind (Hume)." What is commonly called the mind, said Hume, is nothing but a series of unrelated sensations; the word "mind" is only a convenient term for a particular set of sensations that have no substantial causal connection. Thus, "ideas" are simply names (nominalism) for apparent relationships that are no more than customary ways of experiencing and speaking. Hume presents these major hermeneutical notions in *A Treatise of Human Nature* and *Enquiry Concerning Human Understanding*.[23]

Hume is an important and terminal figure who demolishes confidence in the vaunting optimism of the rational autonomous self from the Renaissance to the Enlightenment. Descartes begins the epoch with a philosophical *tour de force* by doubting everything but the *I* who is thinking, soaring from that one certain truth to a whole universe of logical relationships upheld by God himself. Hume falls back to earth in a daze of sensations, doubting that there is any substantial *I* at all. If one cannot know oneself, then other selves or things cannot be known either, nor can God be known. One experiences impressions and ideas but not as an unchanging self, for a person is only a changing bundle or collection of different perceptions. Only successive perceptions constitute the mind. Because of the duration of some of these experiences one may be misled into thinking that the mind has a substantial and continuing identity. Hume's view of the self is therefore like the Buddhist contention that the self is insubstantial and is in reality only a temporary bundle or skein of sensory experiences. These experiences are not even causally related. It is only custom or habit that leads us to suppose that there are causal connections between sensations (although the appeal to custom would seem to suggest an inconsistent argument for causal relationship).[24]

As for God, Hume agreed with the Christian empiricists Locke and Berkeley that the ontological argument of the rationalists was useless, since no knowledge can come from

---

[23]For the complete text of *An Enquiry Concerning Human Understanding*, see Walter Kaufmann, *Philosophic Classics*, 318–414.

[24]Ibid., 325–39.

a priori logic but only from the senses. He repudiated their argument for God from the beauty and order of the world, however, arguing that since there is no spiritual substance, God cannot exist. Even if he did, he would be irrelevant as a first cause because there is no causality in the world. And even if there were, there would be no need for a cause greater than what is precisely adequate to bring about the effect. Since there is no God, there is no heaven or hell and no higher moral law than what evolves from sensory experience alone.[25]

Hume therefore marks the end of the road for radical empiricism, rigorously followed to its logical conclusion. If the rationalists could be dismissed because their competing logical systems seemed to cancel each other out, Hume succeeded at last in eliminating the substantial mind and the self altogether. Unaided empiricism, with its locus of authority in the sensing individual, can give certain knowledge of nothing, certainly not of relations, of togetherness, nor even of the personal *I*, and hardly of God. The hermeneutics of empiricism is, in the last word, thoroughly skeptical and ironical. Beginning with the reduction of all authority to the sensing self, Hume ends with no self at all.

It remained for Kant to try to pick up the pieces and rescue what was salvageable from the ego-centered philosophies of his predecessors, whose speculative ventures catapulted human authority into prominence in the modern quest for a thoroughly autonomous science of interpretation, free of the sovereignty of God and scriptural authority.

THE LEGACY OF KANT (1724–1804)

On the empirical side, Kant's views are similar to Berkeley's to the degree that he adopts the hermeneutics of idealism and empiricism. That is, reality is thought to consist of ideas based on sense experience. But Kant dismisses Berkeley's

[25]See Hume's *Dialogues Concerning Natural Religion*, Norman Kemp-Smith, ed. (New York: Nelson, 1947), 127–228. Also Kaufmann, "Of Miracles," *Philosophic Classics*, 380–94. Hume's repudiation of the God of Scripture is final.

Christian idealism with its referral through the mind of God because it detracts from the autonomy and sufficiency of the human mind. Hume, on the other hand, presents a different set of problems. As an empiricist, Hume agrees with Berkeley that the objects of knowledge are ideas or images that come from one's personal experience. But because he rejects Christianity, he has no access to God as the guarantor of universal images available to all. With Hume the perils of empiricism are fully unveiled: (1) cut off from God, the self can have no certain knowledge of another person's mind, past or present (looking ahead, we can anticipate what effect that will have when empiricist hermeneutical methods are applied to historical and biblical studies); and (2) even more ominous, the self can have no idea of its own mind, for there is no spiritual substance that does the experiencing: the self and other selves are only successive bundles of changing perceptions with no substantial identity.

Kant sought an escape from the skeptical conclusions of Hume by combining what he saw to be the valid insights of British empiricism with the best of rationalist thought from the Continent. He fused the two into a transcendental critique that made the human mind the ultimate source of meaning and understanding. In a hermeneutical revolution as consequential in the realm of ideas as the Copernican revolution in the natural sciences, Kant rejected the notion that truth is correspondence with the mind of God or with a reality external to our knowing. Instead he argued that objective reality can be known only as it conforms to the hermeneutical structures of the knowing mind. Things as they are in themselves (*noumena*) can never be perceived or known; only those things in our experience that appear (*phenomena*) within the categories of our understanding (such as the conceptual grids of space, time, causality, substantiality) can ever be known. Natural events can therefore be known, but only as phenomena or appearances that must be filtered through the patterns of our understanding.[26]

---

[26]This is laid out in Kant's monumental search for an incontestable realm of reason based on human experience, *Critique of Pure Reason*, Norman Kemp-

Accordingly, experiential data are affirmed, as the British empiricists insisted, but only by drawing them through the grid of the experiencing mind, for Kant distances himself from the original Lockean notion that the mind is a simple impressionable blank tablet on which sensations from the objective world impress themselves. In Kant's new system of the transcendental self, the mind determines the way in which the world is perceived. The world can be known only on human terms as it appears to us, never as it is in itself.

As for the other stream that feeds into his thinking, namely the rationalist school of logic and mathematics that comes by way of Leibniz, Kant acknowledges both the value and the limitations of logic and rational thinking by pointing out (ironically with his own calculating logic) that all attempts to embrace the noumenal world in a unified rational system cannot succeed. Rather, all such attempts always end in unresolvable contradictions or antinomies (examples are freedom/determinism, world as finite/world as infinite, God exists/God does not exist, and the like).[27]

Hence, while religious, ethical, and aesthetic experience in the realm of faith affords practical assurance of noumenal reality, as well as universal moral law, God, immortality, and freedom of the will, pure reason itself allows of no ultimate logical system free of antinomies. Thus Kant takes what he considers the best of rationalism and empiricism and locates

---

Smith, trans. (New York: St. Martin's Press, rev. ed. 1933). References are to the standard German edition of Kant's *Gesammelte Schriften*, ed. Koeniglich preussichen Akademie der Wissenschaften, vol. 3: *Kritik der reinen Vernunft: Zweite Auflage*; vol. 4: *Kritik der reinen Vernunft: Erste Auflage* (Berlin: Georg Reimer, 1911). Accepted usage for citations distinguishes the editions: A:1781/B:1787. On the distinction between phenomena and noumena, see A236-60 in Kaufmann, *Philosophical Classics*, 469–80.

[27]See Kant, *Prolegomena to Any Future Metaphysics That Will Be Able to Come Forward as Science*, trans. James W. Ellington (Indianapolis: Hackett, 1977), 80. See also Sadik J. Al-Azm, *The Origins of Kant's Arguments in the Antinomies* (Oxford: Clarendon, 1972); Victoria S. Wike, *Kant's Antinomies of Reason: Their Origin and Resolution* (Washington, D.C.: University Press of America, 1982); Philip M. Hillmer, *The Antinomy Structure of Kant's Transcendental Dialectic* (Atlanta: Emory University, private pub., 1987).

them in separate compartments within the autonomous human mind, where science cannot invade the domain of faith, ethics, and aesthetics, and where the latter cannot invade science. This sets up the Kantian hermeneutical system that has been so influential in nineteenth- and twentieth-century schools of interpretation: the pole of freedom locates the domain of faith and religion, while the pole of causality and determinism identifies the scientific world of time, space, nature, and history. Kant allows neither to influence the other, thus creating a new form of dualism that arises from his agnosticism regarding the claims of the earlier rationalism and empiricism.

Kant therefore comes back, full circle, to the dualism of Descartes whose extreme rationalism he dismisses but whose dualism he replicates in the separation of the free transcendent ego from the realm of nature and history, which is causally determined. The one major difference in Kant's dualism is that he limits both realms to phenomena located in the experience and ideas of the autonomous self. The human ego is now fully in control of the enterprise of meaning and understanding in whatever realm it seeks to explore. By implication, the biblical interpreter who accepts the Kantian dichotomy will confine religious experience to the domain of personal, transcendental faith (which cannot be touched by historical criticism) and confine the historical-critical method to analysis of natural cause and effect without recourse to matters of faith or supernatural revelation.

In *Critique of Pure Reason* Kant argues that our knowledge is composed (1) of experience based on sensory impressions (the empirical or *a posteriori pole*, where propositions are decided only after facts are available) and (2) of categories of the mind that enable us to organize and interpret the world (the rational or *a priori pole*, where the truth or falsity of propositions can be shown by pure reason, prior to observation). The empirical pole cannot give us such ideas as universal and necessary truth or the notions of space and time; hence these categories of thought must come from the mind through pure intuition and are prior to sensory experience.[28] Kant even argued that in addition to *a priori* analytic propositions, which simply analyze the meaning of words, there are also *a priori* synthetic propositions, such as geometrical judgments, that are factually true before observation. But these are widely repudiated today by scientists who point to non-Euclidean geometries that have been developed since Kant's time through empirical observation.[29]

Accordingly, when we speak of Kant's pervasive influence on modern hermeneutics, we are referring to his larger contention that the autonomous rational mind provides the grid of forms or categories through which our sensory experience of the world can be conceptualized. That is to say, for example, that space does not belong to things themselves (*noumena*) or to their relationships, but is the prior subjective form of our mind by which sensory data are perceived and conceptualized as they appear to us (*phenomena*).

Kant's dualism therefore focuses on the two operations of the self: (1) the transcendental ideal, which is the rational realm of ideas (such as time, space, and causality) in the mind and prior to (2) our sensory experience of actual phenomena by which we perceive space as empirically real. Hence, since the world we know is indissolubly linked to the two poles of the rational/empirical self, the independent "thing in itself" (*das Ding an sich*) can never be known by empirical observation. All meaning and understanding must be filtered through the form-grid of the mind and the sensation-grid of the body. In Kant's transcendental phenomenology the self is seen to be autonomous as it arbitrates how the world is perceived and conceived. The only world we can know is the world as it appears *to us*, for it is we who give its appearances shape and meaning. We know only appearances (*phenomena*), never realities in themselves apart

[28]Kant, *Critique of Pure Reason*, A496/B525.

[29]See, e.g., John G. Kemeney's critique of Kant's *a priori* synthetic propositions in *A Philosopher Looks at Science* (New York: Van Nostrand, 1959), 16–17. See also Vern S. Poythress, *Science and Hermeneutics*, "Foundations of Contemporary Interpretation," vol. 6 (Grand Rapids: Zondervan, 1988), 27–37.

from us (*noumena*). God and Scripture play no central role in the foundational hermeneutics of the *Critique of Pure Reason*.

There is, accordingly, a vexing problem that attends the centrality of the transcendental/empirical self in Kant's hermeneutical quest for meaning and understanding. Underlying the system is a skeptical view of things in themselves. Things cannot be known as they really are, not even God. The system also requires an epistemological dualism in which nature/history is determined by the category of cause and effect, rendering objective supernatural biblical revelation in nature and history impossible. The subjective realm of the transcendental ego is reserved as the one area of freedom where the self can experience God, but only subjectively, never objectively or propositionally. The ego is ultimately in control of both arenas. On the one hand, it analyzes nature and history by the deterministic categories of logic, mathematics, and causality that proceed from the mind; on the other, it controls any transcendent experience by the free exercise of the will.

In the development of later liberal theology from Kantian hermeneutics, encounter with God will be confined to the subjective realm, while the Bible will be subjected to naturalistic criticism according to the rational canons of purely historical research. This has had far-reaching consequences in the two hundred years of biblical criticism that followed Kant's dualistic synthesis of rationalism and empiricism.

While there is much in Kant's analysis of meaning and understanding that is brilliantly innovative (the role of the experiencing and conceiving self had never to this point been so carefully examined), the overall effect of his hermeneutical system has been to accord the self an almost absolute status in the determination of the nature of reality. Sensations intuited from the external world are interpreted and given meaning by human categories of understanding. It is we who conceive of experience as it appears *to us*, while things in themselves remain forever beyond our ken. Knowledge is, accordingly, a fusion of the self's sensory and passive intuition of the multifarious and disorganized phenomenal world with pure *a priori* categories of conception. The latter belong to the mind's active faculty of unifying and synthesizing understanding. The mind functions as the center of hermeneutical judgment by imposing conceptual forms of unity and causality on otherwise unrelated and disorganized sensory data. Kant's twelve *a priori* conceptual categories, on which human experience depends and without which there would be sheer chaos, accord the observer hermeneutical pride of place in that the mind does not conform to the objects of knowledge in the world but makes the objects of knowledge conform to the categories of the mind.

Kant assumes that experience cannot supply the categories of organization, as Hume had insisted. The only alternative (excluding general and special divine revelation from God the creator) is to posit the mind as the primary source of meaning and understanding in the world. Or so Kant thought. The Christian would argue from Scripture that God the Creator has implanted modes of knowing in the human mind correlating with the divinely implanted laws and meanings that reside in an objectively real creation; and that both general revelation throughout nature and special revelation in Scripture attest the image of God in the creature as knower. (Thus a biblical view of God and the world includes elements of both idealism and realism, with the heavier emphasis falling on objective realism.)

Kant was aware of a biblically informed theistic epistemology that functions through the omnipresence of God in creation and Scripture, but he rejected it in favor of his own epistemological dualism that accords the human mind and human experience final authority in determining meaning and understanding. Yet in rejecting the creative presence of God, who both posits *a priori* and innate ideas in the mind and correlates these ideas with our experience of the objective external world, Kant was unable to account satisfactorily for the presence of either. For him God operates only on the periphery of his epistemology, in the realm of morality as we will see presently, and as a kind of numinous ground of all that is ultimate. But in his central thought, he insists that reason and experience are sufficient to construct a hermeneutics of meaning through the synthesizing faculty of human imagination without the help of divine revelation.

One of the difficulties of the Kantian system is that instead of God's creating and sustaining space, time, and causality, the self imposes these organizational categories on experience. Yet claiming that external objects in the world must conform to a necessary rule of connection in the mind does not make it so. Kant has not explained why experience of the world and conceptual thought do in fact correlate to the degree that not only ordinary life but the technical sciences as well are made possible. He has taken credit only for the correlation and posited it in the human ego, which replaces God as the real source of the "transcendental unity of apperception," as he calls the process of reasoning and knowing. As for God, we have noted that Kant rejects divine self-revelation in Scripture; in addition, he repudiates the traditional scholastic arguments for God's existence (ontological, teleological, cosmological). God does not necessarily exist, for he cannot be known as an object of truth in propositional terms. This is so because all knowing is based on experience in the sensory world of phenomena—a world that is controlled by the mechanistic law of causality originating in the mind. Thus Kantian hermeneutics rules out traditional metaphysics and theology.

The problem of moral responsibility and free choice now arises for Kant in a world that is totally deterministic. He therefore proposes an *a priori* law of the mind that is objective, necessary, and universal, and that he calls the "categorical imperative": "Act only on that maxim whereby you can at the same time will that it should become a universal law."[30] While this law is a duty, freedom can be deduced from it, Kant insists, for in the moment of deciding whether to assent to the ought of the conscience, one is conscious of being free to choose. In Kant's system, freedom is a rational causality of the will that has only itself as cause, independent of the laws of nature where everything is caused by something else; and it is free of the sovereignty of God.

[30]Quoted in Kaufmann, *Philosophic Classics*, 582, from Kant's *Sämmtliche Werke*, ed. Karl Rosenkranz and F. W. Schubert, vol. 8 (1838). Since the rational nature exists as an end in itself, persons are to be treated as ends, not as means; see ibid., 584.

It is this dualism in Kantian thought that has set the pattern for subsequent hermeneutics to our own day: (1) Nature is formally determined by laws imposed on it by the human mind; thus the scientific study of nature and history, including biblical history, must follow naturalistic patterns of cause and effect; no free or supernatural elements may be allowed to enter into the circle of causality. (2) Freedom lies only in the autonomous will of the ego that is self-caused and responsible to the rational laws of its own nature, such as the categorical imperative. Kant cannot prove the reality of the free self but only assumes the hermeneutical circle he has constructed. Accordingly, the self is a duality that functions in two compartmentalized spheres, both of one's own creation: (1) On the natural and empirical side a person belongs to the physically determined world of phenomena where mechanical and behavioral necessity reigns; (2) on the rational and intelligible side the ego transcends the welter of sensations from the world of experience by autonomously imposing unity and order on it. Hence the self plays the dominant role in unifying experience through the "transcendental unity of apperception," the most basic principle of *Critique of Pure Reason*.[31]

Where does God fit into the hermeneutical circle Kant has drawn? Not in the phenomenal world of nature and history, which is subject to mechanical necessity by the law of causality. Only into the world of aesthetic and subjective imagination can God enter at all, (and then only as an "as if" possibility), and in the ethical realm only as a regulative ethical principle. But never is God the ultimate and metaphysical constitutive principle, and never the sovereign God of Scripture. God is drawn in only as a hypothetical possibility to support the practical demands of morality. For although we cannot know that God exists, we need to live morally "as if" he exists. Beyond that, if God truly exists, he cannot be known as he is in himself any more than the noumenal things in themselves are accessible behind their phenomenal appearances. God and noumena are beyond time

[31]Kant, *Critique of Pure Reason*, A103–10/B130–42; Kaufmann, *Philosophic Classics*, 452–55.

and space and can never become objects available to thought and theology, since the thought-categories of space, time, and causality by which the ego organizes the world apply only to sense objects.

Accordingly, Kantian dualism rules out the possibility that the claims of Scripture are true. It can never be known that God is sovereign, that he is the ultimate creator of all that is, and that he has disclosed himself in nature and history (Ps. 19; Rom. 1:19–23), in his incarnate Son, who is the Logos (John 1:14), and in inspired Scripture (14:26; 2 Tim. 3:16). Hence for Kant the only sphere in which God may be met, if he is to be met at all, is in the transcendent realm of the subjective self with its freedom of will—the realm where no descriptive categories are possible and where no objective truth statements about God can be made. Biblical theology and systematic theology are ruled out and reduced to the subjective immediacy of the transcendent ego. That is why in Kantian hermeneutics one moves to maturity through three levels, from the level of the religion of the masses, through the level of ethical duty, to the highest level of aesthetics. In the final analysis, the transcendent ego functions most freely in the subjective aesthetic sphere. Like Descartes, but with the scale more finely tuned, Kant presents a dualistic hermeneutics in which the scientist (including the biblical historian and theologian) (1) must assume the law of mechanism in making objective statements about the world, an assumption that excludes God's general and special revelation in nature and history, and (2) limits God to the subjective world of the free and transcendent self, where Deity is at most a useful regulative principle but never a constitutive principle and never objectifiable in propositional theological statements.[32]

Kant's dualism passed into nineteenth-century liberal hermeneutics with far-reaching results in biblical interpretation and continues to dominate critical methodologies in biblical studies and theology in the twentieth century, as subsequent

[32]The conviction that God exists is not a logical but a moral certainty, Kant maintains, and rests on the subjective grounds of one's experience, *Critique of Pure Reason*, A:631–42, 820–31; Kaufmann, *Philosophic Classics*, 556–63.

chapters will point out. At the end of the day, Kantian hermeneutics announces that the thinking self is the autonomous ego, the absolute subject of all one's judgments. The transcendental ego is the ultimate arbiter who determines the grounds on which God is allowed, if he is allowed at all, to address the self and the world.

2

THE KANTIAN LEGACY IN THE NINETEENTH CENTURY

PRINCIPAL PHILSOPHICAL SCHOOLS

We have seen how the philosophical foundations for liberal hermeneutics were laid down by Kant at the close of the eighteenth century. The dominant schools of philosophy and biblical interpretation in the 1800s were largely variations on the Kantian synthesis of rationalism and empiricism from the two previous centuries. In this chapter we will examine representative hermeneutical systems of principal nineteenth-century philosophical schools in preparation for later chapters on twentieth-century interactions between philosophical hermeneutics and biblical interpretation. We will observe that Kant's dualistic epistemology, which focuses on the autonomous self (where the phenomena of nature are deterministically ordered by the categories of the mind while the self remains free in its transcendent subjectivity), exerted tremendous influence on nineteenth-century thought, while fostering numerous in-house adaptations and modifications. Kantian hermeneutics is essentially dialectical and unstable, continually oscillating between the pole of deterministic nature and the pole of subjective freedom.

The following sketch of prominent nineteenth-century philosophical schools will afford the reader an overview of the significant inroads Enlightenment thought made on that great century of change through the critical hermeneutics of Kant. Each philosopher/theologian will be seen to emphasize either the objective pole of nature (rational, scientific mechanism) or the subjective pole of the ego (freedom of the will, subjective religious immediacy), or each will attempt to bring the two into some sort of synthesis. In keeping with the autonomous spirit of Kantian hermeneutics, all these philosophical schools reject the full authority of biblical revelation and assume the primacy of human reason and experience in the interpretation of Scripture and in the formulation of theological points of view.

Friedrich Schleiermacher (1768–1834). A German philosopher and theologian of wide influence in nineteenth- and twentieth-century thought, Schleiermacher was an eclectic who was influenced by Spinoza, Kant, and the Romantics Fichte and Schelling. In his major work, *The Christian Faith* (1821–22), as well as in his earlier discourses *On Religion* (1799),[1] he accepted Kant's contention in the *Critique of Pure Reason* that religion cannot be founded on theoretical reason. Nonetheless, he rejected Kant's argument in *Critique of Practical Reason* that it belongs in the ethical realm, suggesting rather that it properly belongs in the aesthetic sphere of Kant's third critique, the *Critique of Judgment.*[2] Like Fichte and Schelling, Schleiermacher was a romantic who favored the subjective pole of freedom in the Kantian dualistic scheme. He defined religion as a feeling of dependence on God, free of traditional doctrine and binding biblical exegesis, and centered on the ego's emotional, aesthetic, and mystical experience of union with God. Spinoza's identification of the self with God was reflected in this romantic pantheistic theology, while the rationalism and semi-deism of Kant were downplayed.

---

[1]Friedrich Schleiermacher, *The Christian Faith* (Philadelphia: Fortress, 1976); idem, *On Religion: Speeches to Its Cultured Despisers*, trans. John Oman (New York: Harper & Row, 1958), Eng. trans. of *Über die Religion: Reden an die Gebildeten unter ihren Beraechtern*, ed. Rudolph Otto (Göttingen: Vandenhoeck und Ruprecht, 1920). See also Schleiermacher, *Hermeneutics: The Handwritten Manuscripts*, AARTT 1, ed. H. Kimmerle, trans. J. Forstman (Missoula, Mont.: Scholars, 1977).

[2]Schleiermacher, *On Religion*, 113.

Schleiermacher reduces the authority of Scripture to the subjective intuition of the autonomous self, as the self mirrors a universe that is one with God. Jesus is but one mediator among many (thereby the door is opened to the comparative study of religion, suggesting a wider "natural religion"). Christ "redeems" by his ethical influence upon the believer, bringing a higher harmony between the infinite and the finite. Bypassing the authority of Scripture and its rediscovery in the Reformation, Schleiermacher asserts that a truly religious person is not one who trusts in Holy Scripture but who really needs no Scripture at all and might himself be able to create scripture out of his own experience.[3] Thus the weight of authority shifts away from inerrant Scripture, revealed and attested by God, to the authority of the self by way of romanticism, pietism, and philosophy of religion. The autonomy principle in Kantian hermeneutics wins an articulate spokesman for liberal theology in Schleiermacher, whose thought widely influenced biblical interpretation throughout the nineteenth and twentieth centuries.

Georg Wilhelm Friedrich Hegel (1770–1831). At the end of the eighteenth century, Kant had brought to a climax the long struggle of previous eras to articulate a comprehensive hermeneutics of meaning, thoroughly humanistic and autonomous and free of traditional biblical authority. Employing Kant's epistemology, but not his individualism, Hegel set out to construct an even more comprehensive agenda. The result was a philosophical theology that dominated the thought of the nineteenth century (and much of the twentieth) and encompassed an impressive range of interests. Whereas Fichte was

---

[3]Ibid., 91. The translator paraphrases the German poorly at this point and softens its radical import. The original text (*Über die Religion*, 76) reads: "Every holy scripture is merely a mausoleum, a deathly reminder that a great spirit who once was there is no longer there. For were he still alive and working, how would such great work lie in dead letters, which give only a weaker impression of himself? One does not have religion who believes in a holy scripture, but who needs none and indeed could make his own" ("Nicht der hat Religion, der an eine heilige Schrift glaubt, sondern der, welcher keiner bedarf und wohl selbst eine machen könnte").

largely concerned with moral issues and Schelling with nature, both being overly romantic and individualistic, Hegel combined morality and nature with religion and a wide range of other concerns, though he remained in many respects a romantic. He placed all these concerns in the context of historical development toward ever higher syntheses. His comprehensive hermeneutical theory describes a universal World-Soul progressively evolving through dialectical stages of thesis, antithesis, and synthesis in an evolution spiraling ever upward. This dialectic is a logical, organic, and all-inclusive unity that nevertheless preserves all differences.[4]

As a sophisticated philosopher of an imagined divine process, Hegel believed that reality is an evolutionary dialectic whose end is logically entailed in the beginning. The Absolute Spirit contains everything and realizes itself progressively as self-conscious and self-knowing Mind. This is the principal theme of Hegel's *Phenomenology of the Spirit*, which attempts to integrate science and the evolution of mind as it progresses through dialectical stages toward the absolute synthesis of universal Mind-Spirit.[5] Hegel's deity is not the personal God of Scripture, nor is his hermeneutical method informed by biblical exegesis. His authority resides in reason and metaphysical speculation. The metaphysical mind posits a universality in which all other persons and objects are aspects of its own processive reflection. The whole world process is accordingly lifted to the status of deity and is viewed as the long journey by which Mind realizes and becomes conscious of itself as "being-by-itself" (*Fürsichsein*).[6] As the individual mind participates in this evolving process of the World-Spirit and allows itself to flow with the logical science of experience, reflecting upon itself as both subject and object, the dialectic of subjectivity and objectivity is finally overcome and the identity of the ego with the Absolute Mind is realized. In the final synthesis, Hegel sees the self as divine and absolute because it is ultimately identified

[4]Hegel, "The Philosophy of History," in *The Philosophy of Hegel*, ed. Carl J. Friedrich (New York: Modern Library, 1954), 21–42.

[5]Friedrich, *Philosophy of Hegel,* 410–15.

[6]Ibid.

with the Absolute. The ego "has itself for its object"[7] because the ego is essentially identified with God.

Such speculative redefining of the Creator/creature relationship carries far-reaching consequences for biblical interpretation, since it relativizes biblical propositions that purport to be universally true because they are revealed by God. In Hegel's system, the documents of Scripture belong to the sphere of historical contingency and relativity. Like any other writings they are subject therefore to historical investigation and must be reconstructed according to the law of natural causality; that is, the Scriptures contain no supernatural revelation. They cannot convey absolute truth. Truth lies in grasping the inner metaphysical necessity of rhythm in the larger historical process, which embraces a smaller phenomenon such as the historical evolution of the Bible and Christian theology. An interpreter of the Bible must not think in terms of Scripture's empirical or material images or in the formal rational propositions of biblical theology but should flow with the conceptual thought that constitutes the phenomenon as pure fact; it is in the very moment of immediate pure relation that I as conscious observer am pure *I* and experience the pure fact as *this*.[8] With one esoteric philosophical stroke, Hegel dismisses the authority of God and Scripture by claiming the self as final authority.

Hegel thus reduces the objective truth of Scripture to the ego's conceptual experience at the pole of Kant's subjective freedom and autonomy. He uses a play on words in the original German to illustrate that in the relationship of self and object (e.g., the Bible), the ego takes pride of place because the object does not have objective meaning (*Meinen*) apart from the understanding that is mine (*meinen*). Employing the hermeneutics of pantheistic idealism, Hegel makes the autonomous self the ultimate authoritative source of meaning and interpretation. All meaning reduces to the ego. The ego is then elevated to the level of deity through identification with the World-Ego. In

---

[7]Ibid., 466. "The self as such, the abstract person, is absolute being," ibid., 505.

[8]Ibid., 489–90, 503–19.

Hegelian hermeneutics, accordingly, all meaning is finally reducible to one's own rational meaning, which is continually flowing and changing in the logical evolutionary dialectical process of experience. Therefore Scripture must submit to the evolving critical schools of rationalistic historical analysis. Of lasting consequence is one's inner perception and understanding of the dialectic of the developing universal Mind in its journey from Pure Being to Absolute Idea. In its development, the Absolute Mind or Spirit (*Geist*) absorbs particular historical religions like Judaism and Christianity and moves them forward toward the absolute religion, and beyond that to the ultimate synthesis achievable only by philosophy. Christianity is therefore only one historical phenomenon among many religions and is relative to its own time and space within the dialectical process of history. In a world of relativities and historical contingencies, Hegel avers that only a metaphysical philosophical belief in absolute universal Mind is rationally viable and avoids the skepticism of Hume.

Because Hegelian hermeneutics rules out absolutes in the changing and contingent realm of history (although history itself threatens to emerge as a substitute absolute), Christianity with its Holy Scriptures cannot be the source of final truth because it too is destined to be synthesized with everything else in the dialectical process toward the ultimate philosophy of all-encompassing Mind. Biblical criticism may therefore be as radical as one wishes; in fact, it is required that it be radical in order to destroy the idolatry of positing absolute truth in anything that is limited to the historical process. We note here Hegel's exegesis of Galatians 4:4 ("When the time had fully come, God sent his Son"): "That saying means that the self-consciousness had risen to those aspects which belong to the conception of the spirit, and to a desire of comprehending these aspects in an absolute manner. . . . The identity of the subject and God entered the world when *the time was fulfilled*; the consciousness of this identity is the knowledge of God as He truly is."[9] While the Bible is to be read for its ethical instruction,

---

[9]Ibid., 867, his italics.

the authority of its salvation imperatives are bypassed by Hegel, as by Schleiermacher his contemporary. The "outer existence" (*Dasein*) that the Absolute gives itself is set forth in the Romantic Art of the history of Christ, which is however not unique to Christianity, but "unfolds itself in all humanity in which the Divine Spirit becomes ever present. . . ."[10]

Consequently, only a philosophically based hermeneutics encompasses everything, including the Bible and theology, within a larger rationalistic metaphysical system, and it alone is worthy of the term "Absolute." In the preface to his *Philosophy of Right and Law* (1821), Hegel claims that "the rational is actual, and the actual is rational."[11] The Hegelian system has therefore been appropriately described as both "panlogism" ("all is rational") and "absolute idealism" (all resides in the Absolute Idea with which the rational self is identified). Essentially, then, the self is deified by linkage with the Absolute Spirit. In this respect, it might be noted, it bears family resemblance to the idealistic and pantheistic metaphysics of Hinduism (and to Christian Science, an eclectic blend of numerous idealisms).

By virtue of the self-deification of the rational ego, absolute truth and reality reside in one's reason, not in things within nature or history. The latter are changing and contingent and are subject to criticism by the detached understanding. The historical world of image (*Vorstellung*), including the biblical image of Christ Incarnate, gives way to rational concept or notion (*Begriff*). Biblical revelation, by which God discloses himself in historical images, is superseded by philosophical metaphysics. The implications for biblical hermeneutics are clear: (1) the Old and New Testaments are only relatively true and are destined to be synthesized with the relative truths of other religions through the inevitable "coincidence of opposites" in the rhythmic dialectic of historical process; therefore

[10]"Lectures on Aesthetics," in ibid., 357. This constitutes Hegel's view of the kingdom of God, which bears little resemblance to Jesus' teaching in the Gospels. See also 368, 374, 381, 388–89 for further examples of Hegel's reinterpretation of the basic Christian concepts of Trinity and incarnation in light of his philosophy of God as Mind.

[11]Friedrich, *Philosophy of Hegel*, 224.

radical historicist criticism of the biblical documents is required; and (2) the final authority for determining the meaning and relative truth of Scripture is the rational ego.

Hegel goes beyond Kant in linking the individual mind with the universal Mind, thereby deifying the rational self. But in other respects the Kantian hermeneutical method is affirmed in Hegel's system of interpretation. The rational ego has authority to interpret not only the empirical realm of nature and history (the pole of science), but also the inner realm of metaphysical meaning and experience (the pole of transcendent freedom). God, Scripture, and theology are all under the control of the rational self, which in turn is one with the Absolute Spirit. The autonomous self becomes the supreme interpreter, the master of meaning. *Meinen* is *meinen*, [“meaning is mine].” That is the essential hermeneutical message of the Enlightenment on a grand scale.

Hegel's hermeneutics of absolute idealism was widely influential in philosophical and theological circles, extending to the English-speaking world through F. H. Bradley (1846–1924) in Britain and Josiah Royce (1855–1916) in America, both of whom established their own circles of influence. On the Continent, the Tübingen New Testament scholar Ferdinand Christian Baur (1792–1860) used the Hegelian dialectic to depict the inner conflict of Petrine and Pauline theologies (thesis, antithesis), with synthesis in the later New Testament documents. Ludwig Feuerbach, meanwhile, advanced the Kantian deconstruction of theology and Scripture by insisting (in *The Essence of Christianity*, 1841; *The Philosophy of the Future*, 1843; and *The Essence of Religion*, 1853) that the idea of God is no more than illusory self-projection of finite humanity attempting to escape its finitude. On the political side, Karl Marx (1818–83) demythologized the spiritual pantheism of Hegel and adopted a hermeneutical materialism, identifying the absolute with an economic dialectic of history. All were but variations on the Kantian theme of the autonomous interpreter and expressions of the Copernican revolution in hermeneutics. We have observed that once the normative absolutes of Scripture are discarded, the autonomous interpreter assumes the role of authority and lays claim to the control of the ultimate grid of meaning.

Søren Kierkegaard (1813–55). In the religious sphere, where church and Scripture were still important but under enormous pressure to conform to modernity, Kant's hermeneutics had a more subtle but no less devastating effect in the two hundred years that were to follow his first *Critique*. Kierkegaard was alarmed by Hegel's massive systematic development of Kantian idealism. But in rejecting Hegelianism he simply fell back to the subjective pole of the Kantian dialectic. He retained enough scriptural allusion to render his writings attractive to later neoorthodox interpreters in the twentieth century who would move, as we will see, in subjectivist reaction against the political social gospel of late-nineteenth-century Ritschlianism and would find the subjective existentialism of Kierkegaard appealing. Little known outside his native Denmark at the time of his writing, Kierkegaard offered the theological world another variation on the hermeneutics of religious subjectivity. His emphasis on the infinite qualitative difference between God and creature heightened subjective experience as the normative point of contact between heaven and earth. This would later negatively influence the interpretation of the Gospels as objective records of the historical incarnation of the Son of God.

While eternity and time intersect in the paradox of Jesus, Kierkegaard's solitary individualism becomes the keynote for understanding biblical faith and appropriating it for oneself. In *Fear and Trembling and The Sickness unto Death*,[12] Kierkegaard offers a panegyric on Abraham as the knight of faith who suspends the ethical for a higher end (*telos*). This is "the teleological suspension of the ethical." In his subjective experience of God, Abraham confronts the paradox of renouncing the universal law against murder in obedience to God who commands him to offer up Isaac. Kierkegaard interprets this to mean that subjective faith takes precedence over the revealed norms of law and Scripture, if one hears the inner voice. Thus

[12]Søren Kierkegaard, *Fear and Trembling and The Sickness unto Death*, trans. Walter Lowrie (New York: Doubleday, 1954), 64–86.

"God and man are two qualities between which there is an infinite qualitative difference."[13] Doctrine contains unfathomable contradictions and paradoxes (Kant's antinomies); accordingly, subjective faith gains pride of place: "By relating itself to its own self and by willing to be itself, the self is grounded transparently in the Power which constituted it."[14]

Although there is much that is novel and exegetically stimulating in Kierkegaard's writings,[15] the overall effect of his hermeneutics encourages imbalance. This is especially true in twentieth-century neoorthodox theology, in which the pole of subjectivity is elevated over objective and rational truth in respect to both general and special revelation.

Albrecht Ritschl (1822–1889). Hegel's grand-scale metaphysical speculations began to lose favor in Germany during the latter part of the nineteenth century, but the critical idealism of Kant remained a powerful force and found expression in less rationalistic variations of his idealism. These followed the lines of Kant's dualistic hermeneutics, which divided the world between the pole of rational-empirical determinism (science) and the pole of subjective freedom and moral value (religion and ethics). Among the most influential neo-Kantians, Albrecht Ritschl had started out as a follower of Hegel and Baur but came to reject their metaphysics as he had rejected the propositional doctrines of classical theology. Whereas Hegel identified being with thinking, and Schleiermacher had given priority to religious feeling, Ritschl emphasized ethical will and action. According to his hermeneutics, Scripture and theology are not concerned with historical and verbal facts but with

---

[13]Ibid., 257.

[14]Ibid., 262.

[15]See, e.g., Søren Kierkegaard, *Works of Love: Some Christian Reflections in the Form of Discourses*, trans. Howard and Edna Hong (New York: Harper & Row, 1964); idem, *Either/Or*, 2 vols., trans. David and Lillian Swenson (New York: Doubleday, 1959); idem, *Selections from the Writings of Kierkegaard*, trans. Lee M. Holland (New York: Doubleday, 1960). See also Edward J. Carnell, *The Burden of Kierkegaard* (Grand Rapids: Eerdmans, 1965), 169–72, for a perceptive criticism of Kierkegaard's disjunction between faith and public evidence, certainty and passion, which follows an appreciative presentation of Kierkegaard's major themes.

functional values and the nonverbal, such as love. Kant's disjunction between the theoretical and the practical, reason and morality, was perpetuated in Ritschl's adaptation of Kantian hermeneutics to Christian experience.[16] For Ritschl, "God is love" sums up the meaning of God. At one pole, theology was reduced to personal faith and moral imperatives, with Jesus as chief exemplar, while at the other pole Scripture was subjected to whatever was demanded by the naturalistic and deterministic methodologies of current historical criticism.

Ritschl attempted to return to the major themes of Scripture and the Reformation, but unlike Schleiermacher, who was so close to the Enlightenment and mystical pietism that he bypassed the Reformation and the biblical doctrine of justification altogether, Ritschl reinterpreted the great biblical and Reformation doctrines of reconciliation and justification as the establishment of a new ethical human community on earth, the kingdom of God.

Thus was born the modern movement popularly known as theological liberalism. From a practical and political point of view, its goal was not altogether unlike that of Hegel or contemporary liberation theologies. Its goal was the moral organization of humankind, ostensibly through a social gospel of love and justice. According to Ritschlian hermeneutics, Scripture does not give factual data about God or Jesus the Son or about the objective nature of reality (these would not qualify as Kant's judgments of fact). Scripture does describe, however, how God and Jesus are for us in the ethical task of realizing the kingdom of God through the reconciliation of human society (Kant's judgments of value). Kant had appealed to practical reason to decree that every human being has been endowed with consciousness of an ethical categorical imperative and possesses the ability to realize its demands. Ritschl perpetuates this functional interest of Kantian hermeneutics and turns a subjective intuition into a universal ethical ideal.

Ritschl's use of Scripture was selective, arbitrary, and

---

[16]Albrecht Ritschl, *The Christian Doctrines of Justification and Reconciliation*, vol. 3 (Clifton, N.J.: New Jersey Reference Book Publishers, 1960), 13.

vulnerable. Subjective feeling about the love and justice of Jesus would not long withstand the assault on the Gospels themselves by radical New Testament scholars at the close of the nineteenth century. Freedom pole and science pole were coming into serious conflict. The instability of Kantian dualism is nowhere more ironically displayed than in the Ritschlian dilemma. Subjective religious experience of the historical Jesus provided the foundation for its idealistic universal social experiment. Yet this was undercut by the other half of the Kantian system with its insistence on naturalistic determinism in scientific and historical studies, rendering Scripture an unstable and unreliable source of truth. By the close of the century, the confident liberal portrait of the historical Jesus was quickly fading under the bright light of early redaction criticism. A widening consensus among more radical Continental scholars was that the Gospels were largely products of evolving churches in the late first century. These churches created much of the Jesus material to meet their current ecclesiastical needs.

Around the corner, Ritschlian utopianism was about to be dealt another blow, against which its Pelagian view of innate human goodness left it defenseless. World War I was to demand hard decisions about human nature: either a retreat from social utopianism into greater subjectivism (pietism, the *Heilsgeschichte* of Barth and the existentialism of Bultmann) or political totalitarianism (Marxism-Leninism, fascism, ultimately liberation theology). The Ritschlian neo-Kantians were to be allowed no easy escape from the circle of their particular kind of religious subjectivity.

Wilhelm Dilthey (1833–1911). Dilthey looms as an important figure in any discussion of hermeneutical method. Much influenced by Schleiermacher and John Stuart Mill, he held to the Kantian disjunction between natural science and moral science (respectively, *Naturwissenschaft* and *Geisteswissenschaft*). According to Dilthey, the former is the domain of things that are observed at a distance and are formally analyzed by mathematical averages. Moral science lies in the personal domain of immediate experience and enables the interpreter to enter into the human phenomena of the past, on analogy of shared experiences with others in the present. Human nature is a constant in the attempt to understand the meaning of the flow of history. But this constant resides in the uniqueness of each individual. The historian draws on his own uniqueness in understanding others, and he understands himself by drawing on their inner experiences. Hence there is communion between present and past that makes exegesis a personal art.[17] This has its own objectivity, but it lies at the existential pole of life where the interpreter is personally involved with the author of the text. It does not occur at the scientific pole of universal law where the interpreter observes dispassionately, though science may impinge upon the art. The fullness of human life in its social and historical manifestations, not nature, is the subject matter of hermeneutics.

This means, of course, that hermeneutics and exegesis can never be definitive, nor theology objective and propositional. Even God is a projection of human inner experience as the interpreter seeks existential self-understanding. This observation conflicts with Dilthey's insistence that human nature is a constant throughout history. Critics of Dilthey complain that he wrongly assumes that all persons think, feel, and will as he would in a given situation, yet contexts differ with their changing questions and answers, and novelty plays a larger role than Dilthey allows.[18] With his hermeneutical principle of *Nacherleben* (reexperiencing), Dilthey describes the historian's task, not as a mere reproduction but as an imaginative re-creation of the past on the basis of a shared sphere of common meaning: it is "the rediscovery of the I in the Thou." This occurs in a threefold process: (1) understanding the viewpoint of the original participants, (2) understanding the understanding of those directly affected by the actions of the original actors, and (3) assessing these events in view of the historian's

---

[17]See H. A. Hodges, *Wilhelm Dilthey. An Introduction*, vol. 3 (London: Kegan Paul, Trench & Trubner, 1944), 238.

[18]See, e.g., Anthony C. Thiselton, *The Two Horizons: New Testament Hermeneutics and Philosophical Description* (Grand Rapids: Eerdmans, 1980), 239-44.

own time and the existential questions he or she brings to the data.[19]

In light of the fact that these three methodological principles are helpful to the Christian interpreter of Scripture, one would perhaps be tempted to find Dilthey a useful ally in formulating a hermeneutical theory of historical interpretation. Dilthey makes it clear, however, that while religious culture is part of the meaning of the past, no one religion or scripture is normative in the overall interpretation of history.[20] He holds that the historian interacts with two horizons, his own and that of the past, as interpreter and author share the affinity of a common human spirit. But he develops this view in a strictly Kantian direction by cutting the interpreter off from any operation of the Holy Spirit as the dynamic link between present and past. The interpretative work of the Spirit in both general and special revelation is dismissed.

However, without a biblical epistemology, does not the Kantian gulf between phenomena (the way the past appears to the interpreter in the present) and the noumena (the way the past really was) remain ultimately unbridgeable? Kant set up an insoluble dilemma that offers no escape from subjectivism. There is nothing in Kantian epistemology that explains how human beings can have common experiences or agree on common symbols and undertakings. Saying it is so (the universal categorical imperative is a case in point) does not make it so or explain why commonality is often experienced. Only a biblically centered hermeneutics can satisfactorily do that. What is required to bridge subject and object, mind and world, past and present, is the interpretive presence of God the

---

[19]See H. P. Rickman, ed., *Patterns & Meaning in History. Thoughts in History & Society: Wilhelm Dilthey* (New York: Harper & Row, 1962), 43–50, 73, for text and commentary on Dilthey's view of the historian and the historical imagination.

[20]Ibid., 28, 56–59. Dilthey's naturalistic historicism does not deny religions their relative sphere of importance, but rejects any absolute religious point of view. Hence, the inspired and authoritative revelation of the Bible is dismissed. Values are intrinsic to an epoch or culture *within* history; there are no objective, universal values outside history. See ibid., 73–74 for Dilthey's text on this hermeneutical point of view, from vol. 7 of the collected works.

creator, sustainer, and redeemer in every act of authentic knowing. He alone provides a sufficient epistemological base for meaning and understanding by interpreting creation through common and special grace. Only on this ground can the fallen creature understand the nature of reality and have any genuine contact with the past.

Dilthey's belief that the historian can enter into the experiences of persons of the past without the bridging work of the Spirit remains a sentimentalism without adequate rational basis. His hermeneutical method cannot gain access to the noumenal reality of a past already perished; nor for that matter does it allow access to the noumenal reality of persons and events in the present. In the end, Dilthey could only attempt to describe the competing worldviews of history, concluding in a thoroughgoing relativism that there is absolute truth in nothing. Only by a great exertion of subjective sentiment does he try to redeem his pessimism by claiming that the flux and relativity of history nevertheless demonstrate the greatness of the human mind.

Dilthey's final word is a Kantian assertion of confidence in the self as autonomous interpreter of history. Yet one must paraphrase the question Plato long ago put to Protagoras the relativist: If man is the measure of all things, and history knows of no absolutes, does history make room for this one absolute, namely, that there are no absolutes? Is it possible to answer absolutely yes or no without a sacrifice of the intellect and of logic? Is it not actually the case that the bottom line of humanistic hermeneutics, whether ancient or modern, is the rejection of the sovereignty of God in the enterprise of meaning and understanding, and the substitution of the sovereignty of human thought, always at the price of a loss of absolutes? By special revelation, Paul discloses that God has endowed world and creature with significance and meaning, yet the creature has suppressed the truth in unrighteousness (Rom. 1:18–32). That, for the Christian interpreter, is the hermeneutical paradox that only biblical revelation and redemption can resolve.

Ernst Troeltsch (1865–1923). A student of Ritschl, and thoroughly imbued with the hermeneutics of Kantian autonomy, Troeltsch early began to see that Ritschlian moralism lacked a metaphysical base. He returned to Hegel to find a rational component to religion, ruling out inspired Scripture and the rational doctrines of classical Christianity. Influenced by Hegel's emphasis on the process of historical dialectic as absolute and by the views of Dilthey that the human spirit is able to interpret the flow and relativities of history by studying its phenomena, particularly the religions of humankind, Troeltsch developed a sociological and relativist approach to the study of religion. He shared the view of the Enlightenment and of Dilthey that no religion could claim absolute and universal validity, because to be historical and to be relative amount to the same thing.[21] Like Hegel, however, and inconsistently, he insisted that Christianity is the most potent and complete among the world's religions, as God realizes himself in a process that moves inexorably toward the final synthesis, God-history being absolute.

Troeltsch compounded the problem of relativism by distinguishing two kinds of causality in the empirical world. One is a causality in nature that is the proper study of natural scientists, the other a causality in history that is the proper study of historians. In spite of his attempt to inject qualitative novelty into the sphere of historical research (natural science simply describes variations in the quantitative patterns of natural energy), Troeltsch failed to escape the determinism of the Kantian system. In the Kantian system the rational mind overlays deterministic patterns of meaning upon the disordered empirical data of experience. The following principles in Troeltsch's historical methodology are illustrative in this regard and reveal how radically antithetical they are to biblical Christianity:[22]

1. The first principle in his method is *historical criticism*. The historian stands over against historical documents and

---

[21]See Ernst Troeltsch, *The Absoluteness of Christianity* (Richmond: John Knox Press, 1971).

[22]Ernst Troeltsch, "Üeber historische und dogmatische Methode in der Theologie," in *Gesammelte Schriften*, vol. 2, *Zur religiösen Lage, Religionsphilosophie, und Ethik*, 2d ed. (Aalen: Scientia, 1962), 729–953.

controls the open-ended process of interpretation, assuming that interpretation is always historically relative and therefore never more than probable. Hence Christianity cannot claim a final and absolute word on the meaning of history, and Scripture is as subject to historical criticism as any other historical document. There are no inspired documents exempt from historical criticism, since all are controlled by laws of natural causality imposed by the mind.

2. The second principle is that of *analogy*. In the science of historical criticism, this is parallel to the principle of uniformitarianism in the natural sciences. Its operating presupposition is that nothing could have occurred in the past that does not have its analogous counterpart in the present. The present unlocks the past. Since supernatural occurrences are not observed to occur in the present, it must be assumed that none occurred in the past. Classical biblical Christianity must therefore be desupernaturalized to allow historical criticism to describe what really happened in the natural stream of events.

3. The third principle is *correlation* or *causality*. This is the presupposition that all events in history form an interrelated causal nexus in the evolutionary process (Troeltsch here overrides his prior distinction between natural and historical causality). All events are to be interpreted as of the same order, as threads woven of the same web; everything is immanent and interrelated in a naturalistic continuum. Hence, as a corollary of principle 2, no special revelation of a sovereign God is possible in the causal network of history. The supernatural revelation of God in Scripture is effectively desacralized and brought under the control of the critical faculties of autonomous thought, which frames the questions and gives the answers.

With the supernatural ruled out of the arena of history, religious ideas are necessarily relegated to the subjective pole of experience, as Kant had insisted earlier. At the subjective pole the self remains in control of religious experience as well. Where Kant had inconsistently claimed that universal ethical norms such as the categorical imperative may be generated from this "practical" pole (although they are not to be construed as propositional disclosures from a supernatural God), Troeltsch offered no absolute ethical norms. The sphere of subjective religious experience remained for him a matter of personal conviction. In this realm there were no objective-scientific rules to determine truth. While the principle of correlation as applied to the history of religions may reveal similar patterns in the development of human personality, Christian ethics offers little help to the modern age.[23]

As Troeltsch grew increasingly skeptical about the possibility of discovering any absolutes beyond the all-encompassing absolute of history, he completely abandoned the supernatural and historical foundations of Christianity, finally exchanging his professorship in theology for the faculty of philosophy.

CONCLUDING REFLECTIONS ON EIGHTEENTH-AND NINETEENTH-CENTURY PHILOSOPHICAL HERMENEUTICS

In view of the preceding reflections, it is important to note that the Christian scholar should have no quarrel per se with rationalism, empiricism, and religious experience, for these are dimensions of the created world through which God communicates meaning. A comprehensive Christian philosophy that works from God's authoritative disclosure of himself in creation and in Scripture will lay claim to the positive role of rational thinking, sensory experience, and spiritual communion with God.

Problems arise when the human interpreter claims autonomy or "self-rule" in the quest for truth and claims the right to determine the nature of reality without reference to God's interpretation as Creator in general and special revelation. Kant is a philosophical figure worthy of careful scrutiny because he inherited the independent spirit of rationalism and empiricism that characterized the philosophers of the sixteenth and seven-

---

[23]See Ernst Troeltsch, *Die Bedeutung der Geschichtlichkeit Jesus für der Glauben* (Tübingen: Mohr, 1929). See also his article, "Historiography," in John Macquarrie, ed., *Contemporary Religious Thinkers* (London: SCM, 1968), 76–97, reprinted from James Hastings, ed., *Encyclopedia of Religion and Ethics*(1913), 6:716-23.

teenth centuries and brought them together in a humanistic dualism that was to influence the nineteenth and twentieth centuries profoundly.

Not all of Kant's contemporaries and successors in the eighteenth and nineteenth centuries adopted his critical system wholesale. As free thinkers they modified or highlighted various aspects of his critical work. Yet the majority, especially the prominent figures of influence we have examined, tacitly assumed his hermeneutical method of placing human experience and reason above all other authority. Scriptural revelation was systematically deconstructed of its objectivity by radical historical criticism and was reduced to the subjective realm of religious experience; it was hence relativized and brought under the control of the autonomous self.

While the study of Kant, together with his predecessors and successors, can prove to be a fascinating and lifelong undertaking, the Christian scholar will want to seek the gift of spiritual discernment (1 Cor. 12:10) to distinguish truth from error. From a biblical perspective, the discriminating critic can see images of common grace in the school of idealism, since the human mind is endowed with the power of thought and reason to organize in meaningful patterns the sensory experiences of the body in the empirical world. Both the rational and the empirical are valid components of human experience. This is attested by the biblical doctrine of creation, which describes a real world that comes into being by command of God, the source of all intelligence. God endows creation with built-in meaning and appoints the highest of his creatures, who are made in his image, to think his thoughts after him and to superintend creation in orderly fashion (Gen. 1). Idealism therefore contains considerable truth, in that the human mind has powerful reasoning capacities capable of conceptualizing complex patterns of meaning God has placed in the world.

The idealism of the Enlightenment goes radically awry, however, in its rejection of the biblical doctrine of creation and in its refusal to give thanks to God or to honor him as the source of the imaging power of the human mind (Rom. 1:21). Paul makes clear in this important hermeneutical passage that creation is already interpreted by the sovereign creating God, even to the extent of asserting that the eternal power and deity of God's invisible nature are clearly perceived in the things that have been made. But God's witness has been suppressed by a willful and sinful humanity whose "thinking became futile and their foolish hearts were darkened. Although they claimed to be wise, they became fools. . . . They exchanged the truth of God for a lie, and worshiped and served created things rather than the Creator" (Rom. 1:21, 25).

This is a frank assessment of the ambiguous status of the human mind since the fall of humanity recorded in Genesis 3. On the one hand, the image of God in humankind remains such that God's self-revelation and interpretation of creation "has been clearly perceived in the things that have been made. So they are without excuse" (Rom. 1:20). On the other hand, the failure of human beings to honor God or give thanks to him has led to the great exchange of the truth about God for a lie (v. 25), so that they are now futile in their thinking and darkened in their foolish hearts (v. 21), fools (v. 22), and given up by God to an unacceptable mind (v. 28) that does not pass the test of his wisdom and righteousness.

Accordingly, one who honors Scripture as the trustworthy Word of God in respect to the nature and status of creation will honor God and give thanks to him for the gifts that continue to come by way of his common grace, many of them through the divinely endowed human mind. The discerning Christian will also observe where arrogant rebellion against God misconstrues the truth and substitutes the creature for the Creator. Among the predecessors of Kant, Berkeley was the closest to understanding the proper function of ideas. As a Christian he understood that the perception of objects via mental concepts is really perceiving the world through the mind of God. Although his empirical idealism has weaknesses (he is too fascinated with the priority of ideas in the perceiver's mind and not attentive enough to the reality of the objective creation God creates and sustains), he is in a much better position than Kant and his successors to explain why human beings universally experience similar concepts that can be translated in the dynamic equivalents of many languages. The biblical view is that it is due primarily to the image of God reflected in the experience and thought of his creatures and in the intercommunication between objects and selves that is made possible by his common grace in creation.

We will see in subsequent chapters how the philosophical hermeneutics that impact biblical interpretation in the twentieth century remain deeply ingrained by a Kantian dualism that accords priority to the autonomous self, not only in the sphere of religious experience but also in the scientific sphere of inquiry where nature and history are interpreted. In both compartmentalized areas the human will that is in rebellion refuses to acknowledge the objective reality of authoritative Scripture and God's objective revelation in creation that addresses the senses and the mind with his primal interpretation. What is lacking in modern liberal hermeneutics (especially in European idealism and its counterparts in the English-speaking world) is a biblically based philosophical realism that attests a reality beyond the human mind and which communicates itself to human observers through the network of discourse built into it by God who creates and sustains it by his word of power (Heb. 1:3). Wherever humanity goes, wherever it looks, whatever it experiences, God is there sovereignly sustaining and interpreting the universe (Ps. 19:1–6; 139; Rom. 1:20).

The destructive effects of humanistic rationalism, empiricism, and idealism have been realized in modern times, not because these dimensional perspectives are intrinsically bad (they are valid and complementary perspectives of God's creation), but because they have been elevated to the level of hermeneutical autonomy by way of human reason and experience. The fallen and autonomous ego has assumed the prerogative of fashioning reality in its own image, a right that belongs to the Creator alone. In his own day Isaiah severely rebuked his people for their false idealism and described with biting irony their penchant for fashioning idols according to their own imaginative ideas (Isa. 44:9–20). The ironsmith forges a god of iron over coals; the carpenter sketches and shapes a block of wood into the figure of a man, with the beauty of a man, and worships a block of wood that comes from the same tree that provides wood for warmth and wood for baking bread. God brings an ironic curse upon such idolaters, for what seems to them to be rationally and empirically grounded idealism (iron, wood, and fire do after all provide operational power—why not worship them?) is in God's eyes folly and leads to loss of ability to discern the nature of reality:

> They know nothing, they understand nothing; their eyes are plastered over so they cannot see, and their minds closed so they cannot understand. No one stops to think, no one has the knowledge or understanding to say, "Half of it I used for fuel; I even baked bread over its coals, I roasted meat and I ate. Shall I make a detestable thing from what is left? Shall I bow down to a block of wood?" He feeds on ashes, a deluded heart misleads him; he cannot save himself, or say, "Is not this thing in my right hand a lie?" (Isa. 44:18–20)

This realistic biblical view has significant hermeneutical implications. Biblical realism does not deny the importance of ideas in the mind. Indeed, it affirms, as in the Isaiah passage above (as does Jesus on the significance of inner thoughts, Mark 7:14–23) that persons fashion their world imaginatively within their minds, intend that world to be universally true, and attempt to order their actions according to that imagined world. Idealism is therefore not only a valid but an inescapable function of the human mind. Being made in the image of God means thinking his thoughts after him and conforming one's actions to those thoughts. But precisely here the substantial difference between biblical idealism and humanistic idealism can be discerned. Biblical idealism is grounded in the belief that truthful ideas have their origin in the primordial ideas of God, not in the human mind. Accordingly, they are ultimately referential to the creative thoughts and acts of God. God's universe therefore has real existence, and because of his presence in framing creation, this reality communicates its noumenal (real), not just its phenomenal (apparent) meaning to the human mind through the empirical senses. Idealism, realism, rationalism, and empirical experience accordingly complement one another, since the objective reality of God has priority. This epistemology is much superior to the Kantian view which inevitably founders on the unknowability not only of God, but also of objective things in themselves, other selves, and in the end, even one's own self.

The nineteenth century came to a close, as we have seen, with a heady kind of historical relativism born of the optimism of the age, represented by the internally unstable hermeneutics of Dilthey and Troeltsch. One can appreciate their interest in history and learn much from their historical methodology without succumbing to their Hegelian absolutizing of process and human thought, and their virtual deification of the human drama. Analysis of history is required of the scholar; but for the biblically oriented interpreter, history does not have intrinsic worth and cannot function as an absolute. In light of Scripture, history is part of created space-time and serves as the medium of God's self-revelation and redemptive work, which eventually redeems history from its convoluted rebellion. Only in the incarnate Son of God does history find its fulfillment and its redemption from the curse of entropy brought upon it by the Fall (Rom. 8:20). In order to gain objective truth about history's meaning and the larger meaning of creation, authoritative Scripture is indispensable. But it was precisely the infallibility of Scripture that was under attack in the rationalistic and empirical philosophies leading up to the Enlightenment and in the hermeneutics of Kant and his successors from the Enlightenment on to the end of the nineteenth century.

Nothing was to change in the academic world of criticism with the dawning of the twentieth century. Indeed, the speed with which historicist and relativist hermeneutics gathered momentum at the turn of the century is a story to be told elsewhere. It is replete with warnings for the present. Hundreds of colleges and scores of theological seminaries once faithful to historic Christianity and to biblical realism became liberal and Kantian in orientation. Much is to be learned from the trends of hermeneutical thought in the twentieth century, and some can be turned to advantage as they offer fresh insights into old themes, provided one uses them cautiously and judiciously (several such applications are made in the present study).

But we should observe that in spite of contemporary criticisms of Kant from secular scholars, to whom he is particularly vulnerable (e.g., physical scientists have rejected his simplistic notions about the ranges of scientific theory), such criticisms are for the most part in-house. For the modern mind, which has discarded God and his interpretation of reality, there is no going back beyond Kant. Dismissing the objective claim of Scripture to represent the true meaning of creation from the divine perspective, modern secular thought has been thrown back on its own resources to interpret reality autonomously. Kant demonstrated the fact that without infallible Scripture as the source of objective truth about the origin, nature, and destiny of humanity and history, only the human mind is left to create the categories of meaning by which human beings are to live out their existence. Kant performed a valuable service in demonstrating that apart from God's revelation in Scripture, the human mind is bedeviled by relativism and skepticism. In his system there is no possibility of knowing the truth about things in themselves or the ultimate meaning of the universe. Such meaning can only be imagined hypothetically by the autonomous human mind acting either singly or collectively in philosophical, economic, political, scientific, or religious enterprises "as if" they were true.

If, in view of modernity's rejection of the authoritative Scripture of historic Christianity, it is impossible to go back beyond Kant, is it possible to go forward beyond Kant? The remaining chapters of part 1 will examine representative influential twentieth-century philosophers who attempt to understand reality without regard to the authority of infallible Scripture, and yet try to solve the Kantian problems that arise in regard to interpretation and meaning. These are principally schools of idealism on the Continent (phenomenology, existentialism, structuralism, neo-Hegelianism) that carry on the idealist trends of German Kantian hermeneutics. Part 1 will conclude with a practical exegetical application of the relational models of Gabriel Marcel, the French existentialist Christian philosopher. Part 2 will examine Anglo-American schools of analysis that emphasize their particular tradition of empirical realism. The leading question to be kept in mind is whether any of these attempts to go forward beyond Kant achieve anything new in the way of hermeneutical certainty, or whether they offer only variations on his fundamental dualism, where meaning and interpretation divide into scientific determinism in the sphere of nature and history, and subjectivity in the sphere of religious experience.

3

TWENTIETH-CENTURY CONTINENTAL IDEALISM

The twentieth-century European philosophies that have most deeply influenced New Testament scholars and theologians have been largely idealist in nature. Advances in the empirical sciences had proven so great, yet so provisional and subject to revision by the turn of the century that critical biblical scholars found themselves searching for reinforcements of the Kantian hermeneutical model, which was still accepted as basically sound. The critical academy continued to pursue an empirical study of the Bible along Kantian lines at the behavioral pole of scientific research, analyzing the biblical documents under the scrutiny of naturalistic assumptions. At the same time, an unsettling principle of indeterminacy began to intrude itself into scientific theory and practice, and this led to constant historical revision and skepticism.

This uncertainty at the science pole tended to affirm increasing suspicion that the historical-critical method could not serve as the foundation of religious certainty. Certainty must be found (assuming the Kantian hermeneutical dualism as a given) in the practical and existential realm at the pole of personal religious experience in direct subjective encounter with God. Emerging atheistic idealist philosophies would describe this subjective experience as the deep encounter of the self with phenomenal essences or with Being that transcends the relativities of history and science. Among these varied attempts to escape the relativity and revisionism of the empirical sciences at the opening of the twentieth century were the new schools of phenomenology, existentialism, structuralism, and neo-Hegelianism. This chapter will examine leading proponents of these contemporary variations on the theme of Kantian idealism.

Phenomenology: Edmund Husserl (1859–1938). One of the most influential European philosophers to set forth an ambitious agenda for twentieth-century hermeneutics, Husserl sought for certainty through a scientific application of phenomenology. The search for certainty, he argued, could not be undertaken through the physical sciences, which were in great flux, nor through the new sciences of historical research and psychology, which were even more unstable in theory and methodology. The quest must be made, Husserl reasoned, by way of a purely descriptive phenomenological science devoid of presuppositions or biases. This would allow the pure essences of self-experience to be described without any taint from the factual world of space-time nature and history.[1] In some ways like Plato (but, importantly, pursuing phenomenal rather than noumenal essences), Husserl sought certain knowledge of universal essences through the science of "eidetic" (beholding) description, describing only what was seen by the beholding eye as it intuited pure phenomena within the experiencing self. The science of intuiting pure phenomena was to be achieved, Husserl argued, by a process of *epochē* or suspension of judgment that brackets everything extraneous to the universal essence, including even the existence of the individual object itself that is under observation. Thus the pure essence of "the phenomenon in itself," as experienced by the conscious ego, could be described without distortion.[2]

Readers may recognize a familiar strain in this methodology, which appeared in the gnostic hermeneutics of second-

---

[1]Edmund Husserl, *Ideas* (New York: Macmillan, 1931). For selections from chapters 1 and 2, see William Barrett and Henry D. Aiken, eds., *Philosophy in the Twentieth Century: An Anthology*, vol. 2 (New York: Random House, 1962), 171–205. See also Paul Ricoeur, *Husserl: An Analysis of His Phenomenology* (Evanston: Northwestern University Press, 1967).

[2]Barrett, *Philosophy in the Twentieth Century*, pp. 178–79.

century sectarians. These interpreters virtually removed the figure of Jesus Christ from the realm of history in order to gain access to the Christ-essence through an intricate process of gnostic higher knowledge, reserved for the few. Rudolf Bultmann, a prominent hermeneutical figure in the Heideggerian-existentialist school (to be considered presently), reflects something of this Husserlian idealism and its Cartesian/Kantian dualism. In his application of New Testament criticism, he undercuts the relevance of the factual biblical data for religious experience by bracketing all objectification of God as idolatry, focusing rather on the pure "essence" of the kerygma of proclamation, which leads to the immediate encounter of the self with God. This occurs apart from dependence on the redemptive work of Jesus Christ in objective history, since Jesus as a historical figure belongs to the Old Testament era. Furthermore, history is subject to relativity and cannot be a medium for absolute revelation. *That* Jesus was is all we need to know; *what* he was is subject to historical criticism and must perforce be bracketed in order to intuit directly the meaning of the essential phenomenon of "Christ" through direct encounter with God. Other elements in Bultmann's hermeneutics will be discussed later, but his similarity to Husserl's version of Kantian idealism needs to be noted at this point.

Phenomenology can be a valuable tool for exegesis when it seeks to describe essential structures in biblical faith.[3] The weaknesses of the school must be observed as well. First to be noted is Husserl's suspicion of the "factual" sciences that deal with nature, history, and psychology because they are limited to space-time and therefore give uncertain results. His attempt to formulate a science of absolute certainty by intuiting and then describing the phenomena of experience directly and purely is difficult to understand, however. While the scholar should try to keep an open mind in any scientific investigation, it is unlikely that anyone is capable of eliminating all presuppo-

[3]Note, e.g., the subtitle of the present writer's study on the Gospels: *New Approaches to Jesus and the Gospels: A Phenomenological and Exegetical Study of Synoptic Christology* (Grand Rapids: Baker, 1982); see esp. chaps. 1, 5.

sitions. Bultmann himself conceded the point that presuppositionless exegesis is impossible.[4] The attempt to practice presuppositionless phenomenology by bracketing the spatiotemporal existence of an observed object is itself based on the radically unbiblical presupposition that (1) nothing in nature and history is capable of affording certain and objective knowledge and (2) does not already contain God's interpretation embedded in creation.

Husserl's gnostic phenomenology claims to intuit only transspatial and transtemporal essences beheld by the transcendent human ego. Ironically, the claim that this phenomenological quest is a purely *descriptive* science actually accords it public status in the marketplace of human discourse, where "nonspatial and nontemporal essences" must be described in space and time. Since public language is bound up with space-time images, any attempt to bracket the temporal existence of an object in order to intuit its pure essence as a phenomenon in human consciousness would be purely private and incommunicable. Husserl wants to return to the historical realm of existence to describe his intuition of essences publicly, without explaining how the terms and experiences of the two realms tie together (this is the question of univocality, or correlation of different levels of discourse, which Husserl does not satisfactorily address). The method therefore betrays illogicality and illustrates further the hermeneutical problems inherent in Kantian dualism.

In this regard, historic Christianity has a decided advantage. Scripture discloses that the special revelation of salvation in Jesus Christ can be proclaimed meaningfully in the public arena because nature itself is already interpreted by God. It is God's act of creation that affords points of contact (univocality) between the language of special grace and the language of common grace. Husserl has no such advantage and can speak only in complex and ultimately meaningless language that he is

[4]Rudolf Bultmann, "Is Exegesis Without Presuppositions Possible?" in *Existence and Faith* (London: Collins, 1964).

intuiting essences with no location in the public world of experience and discourse.

Husserl's hermeneutics is accordingly Cartesian and Kantian in origin, since it is based on a methodology of radical doubt and criticism. The *epochē* is a bracketing or deconstruction of externals where one doubts every spatio-temporal relationship in order to arrive at what is absolutely certain. Descartes posited the autonomous ego of the thinking self as the ground of certainty, yet he did not seem to consider that thinking in French and Latin constituted him a communal human being, who should have thought, "I am in relation; therefore I think." Husserl, similarly, translated his intuitions into complex German. Kant did not appear to question the irrationality of his flight from the realm of the rational-empirical (with its ambiguous antinomies) to the realm of practical reason with its functional appeal to universal maxims of ethical action (the categorical imperative). Husserl's dualism and its focus on the primacy of the ego are even more irrational, for his appeal is to a descriptive science of phenomena removed from the empirical world and accessible only to the self as it plumbs the depths of its own consciousness. Husserl should have been speaking of noumena, the things-in-themselves, and the noumenon of the self as experiencing agent, since phenomena, on the Kantian model, are only the appearances of unattainable noumena as they are experienced in the space-time world. Consequently, although Husserl's method bears superficial similarity to Plato, Plato actually focuses on the objective reality of essences (noumena) which are external to the self, while Husserl pursues phenomenal essences within the subjective realm of the conscious ego. One is dealing, then, only with humanly interpreted appearances.

Husserl wanted to bracket the space-time world and explore the pure phenomena of the experiencing self. Since the self is inextricably bound up with the world of space-time, however, as Heidegger was to insist (and as Husserl was later to concede), Husserlian hermeneutics undertook a flawed enterprise from the start. The weakness and illogic of German idealism are accordingly accentuated by Husserl's attempt to discover the essences of appearances by bracketing the world of appearances and then publicly describing these phenomenal essences "purely and scientifically" to others by means of the language of the world of appearances. Although the method of phenomenology has been widely acclaimed and adopted as a method for objectively describing the similar (synchronic) structures of religious experience and world religions (so structuralism, to be discussed presently), scholarship has not been able to validate Husserl's original program of exploring and describing essential structures by bracketing space-time existence.

We should note again that Husserl's project was to describe the experiences of the conscious *self* (to coin a word, *egology*), not the essence of God or the world as objective fact. Husserl describes his ego-centered hermeneutics in the following terms:

> I myself or my experience in its actuality am *absolute* Reality (*Wirklichkeit*), given through a positing that is unconditional and simply indissoluble. The thesis of my pure Ego and its personal life, which is "necessary" and plainly indubitable, thus stands opposed to the thesis of the world which is contingent.[5]

This is simply Kantian hermeneutics in another key.[6] It can play no substantial role in any biblical exegesis that is faithful to the revelational and propositional claims of Scripture.

Employed as a more humble methodology to describe (however imperfectly) the basic structures of conscious experience in various areas of research, phenomenology can prove to be a useful enterprise. In a more specialized manner, as applied, for example, to the study of Jesus in the Gospels, it can be valuable as a reminder that the scholar needs to bracket prejudicial presuppositions that arise from naturalistic views of the world and distort the essential supernaturalistic intention of Jesus and the reportage of the evangelists. The danger of the phenomenological method is that in seeking to be value-free in

---

[5]Husserl, in Barrett, *Philosophy in the Twentieth Century*, 204. His emphasis.

[6]"Husserl *did* phenomenology, but Kant *limited* and *founded* it." Ricoeur, *Husserl: An Analysis*, 201. His emphasis.

describing the pure structures of conscious experience, it may in fact assume a value-laden worldview that prejudices the outcome and misleads the investigator as well as the reader into thinking that it is producing pure, objective scientific truth from human experience alone. In regard to biblical hermeneutics and exegesis, it is only by allowing Scripture to speak out of its own authority as "pure phenomenon" that the application of phenomenology is justified and valuable. If one is accurately describing the phenomenon of Jesus as portrayed in the Gospels, and not simply adapting him to fit modern naturalist presuppositions, the miraculous and supernatural must be allowed to play their significant roles. The purest and truest phenomenological hermeneutics for biblical exegesis will accordingly allow the phenomena of the Scriptures to make their own case and establish their own horizon of presuppositions, before critical presuppositions that could prove inimical and distorting are applied (these need in turn to come under the scrutiny of Scripture).

For example, in *New Approaches to Jesus and the Gospels*[7] I have resisted applying Troeltsch's historicist reductionism, which would explain the origin of the Gospels in wholly naturalistic terms. Instead, I have assumed that however the Holy Spirit inspired the Gospels to be written in their present form, their authors claim from eyewitness evidence that Jesus typically spoke and acted in these selected patterns of address and asserted remarkable claims to divine authority (John 14:26 is a key text describing the phenomenon of the Spirit's role in recollection and teaching). By these historical speech-acts Jesus offers an objective interpretation of the human condition and inaugurates the divine plan to redeem it.

This hermeneutical program is firmly established on a careful historical/grammatical study of the biblical texts, which are assumed on their own testimony to be divinely inspired and historically objective. Exegesis is therefore not a search for the pure essence of Jesus Christ apart from his incarnate existence,

[7]See esp. the Introduction, which sets forth the hermeneutical assumptions of the study.

as the Husserlian method would require (gnosticism). Philosophical reduction or bracketing (*epochē*) is a valuable tool for exegesis if the interpreter brackets the right thing—namely, those critical presuppositions that would set out to interpret the gospel portraits of Jesus largely as creations of the church with minimal historical content. In this respect the lay believer is in a better position (phenomenologically speaking) to be confronted by the real Jesus of the Gospels than the interpreter who comes to the text with Cartesian doubt and radical Kantian criticism. The critic who doubts does so because he or she is bracketing the wrong material and the wrong set of assumptions. Instead of bracketing the phenomenon of the Jesus of the Gospels, who is represented by the testimony of the evangelists, radical criticism should bracket its own presuppositions, when it does not allow the phenomenon of Jesus to be what, in the gospel accounts, he claims to be. Such phenomenology becomes an intellectual exercise in affirming the rejection of the historical witness of the earliest Christians and the claims of its principal figure.

Hence the bracketing process of the philosophic *epochē* is itself a presuppositional operation. That this is the case with Husserl and his successors can be seen in the phenomenological studies of those who have been influenced by his method. The publications of Rudolf Otto, Gerardus van der Leeuw, Mircea Eliade, and Joseph Campbell[8] aim at singling out archetypal essences in world religions that appear in the religious consciousness. Although valuable in a limited sense, these studies tend to oversimplify the data by bracketing out those concrete (and often offensive) historical distinctives that define the vitality of living faiths as historical phenomena. While aiming ostensibly at objective and scientific description of religious experience, the general application of phenomenological herme-

[8]See Rudolf Otto, *The Idea of the Holy* (London: Oxford University Press, 1923); Gerardus van der Leeuw, *Sacred and Profane Beauty* (New York: Holt, Rinehart & Winston, 1963); Mircea Eliade, *Myths, Dreams, and Mysteries: The Encounter Between Contemporary Faiths and Archaic Reality* (London: Collins, 1968); Joseph Campbell, with Bill Moyers, *The Power of Myth* (New York: Doubleday, 1988).

neutics tends to be subjective and reductionist in its attempt to distill abstract essences from historical religious phenomena. (The similarity of structuralism to Husserlian phenomenology with preference for synchronic essences over diachronic historical processes will be noted later in this chapter.)

To sum up, the Kantian origin of phenomenology is seen to lie in its location of religious experience at the subjective pole of the self, not at the objective pole of authoritative divine revelation in nature and history. This is confirmed by the fact that it is the phenomena of the ego's pure consciousness, not the independent noumena of objective reality, that comprise the subject matter of its descriptive science. In Kantian hermeneutics the "things in themselves" can never be known. The various schools of phenomenology that derive from Husserl are therefore primarily variations on the theme of Kantian idealism, not of realism as is sometimes suggested, though the tension between idealism and realism in Husserl's phenomenology is a real one. It may be briefly noted that one of the best-informed French historians of phenomenology, Paul Ricoeur (whose writings will be discussed later in this chapter), has written penetratingly of Husserl and noted some of the criticisms offered above;[9] e.g., (1) one cannot bracket one's body or the world, as Husserl tried to do; (2) Husserl's preoccupation with the absolute transcendental ego raises problems with the existence of the Other (God or other human beings); and (3) attempts to do the first and the second lead to solipsism, for only the ego, Husserl asserted, is constituted primordially.[10] In his later writings, Husserl's transcendental idealism underwent a profound revision that led him to ground his absolute in the

---

[9]Ricoeur, *Husserl: An Analysis*.

[10]Ibid., p. 11. One might mention here also E. D. Hirsch, who is correct in claiming that a text is to be identified with the author's intended purpose; but he cannot sustain the argument by falling back on Husserl's view of intentionality. See E. D. Hirsch, *Validity in Interpretation* (New Haven: Yale University Press, 1967); idem, *The Aims of Interpretation* (Chicago: University of Chicago Press, 1976). See also Walter Kaiser, *Toward an Exegetical Theology* (Grand Rapids: Baker, 1981), p. 33; Tremper Longman III, *Literary Approaches to Biblical Interpretation* (Grand Rapids: Zondervan, 1987), 20, 25, 67.

primordial evidence of the world. No longer is the monadic ego the irreducible absolute; the absolute is now to be seen as the totality that is prior to all reduction and cannot itself be reduced—namely, the ego and the world in which it is engaged.[11] This is precisely Heidegger's place of beginning and his fundamental difference with the earlier Husserl.

Nontheistic Existentialism: Martin Heidegger (1889–1976). Existentialism is a widely influential contemporary school of hermeneutics, emanating in part from Kierkegaard and the subjective anxiety of the self. It seeks to move away from the restraining patterns of the past into the novelty and freedom of the future through a rigorous decision of the will. The Greek root of the term "existential" (*ek* + *histēmi*) means literally "to stand outside" the past into the next moment of decision, as the self "becomes" more oneself in successive moments of choice. Whether one lives authentically or inauthentically depends on the quality of the decision, and is particularly evident in times of great upheaval and anxiety. It is therefore not surprising to find its fuller expression in settings of forlorn love, as in Kierkegaard's case, or among the twentieth-century philosophers and theologians of war-torn Europe.

Although Kant on his metaphysical side seems far removed from the concerns of existentialism, his dualistic system nevertheless sets up the conditions of the school. Existentialists feel strongly threatened by the deterministic structures of the nature/history pole and, like the phenomenologists, ground their hermeneutics in the Cartesian/Kantian concept of freedom in which an analysis of the phenomena of the self is paramount. Following the descriptive phenomenological methodology of Husserl, but without bracketing the world in pursuit of untainted essences, Martin Heidegger set out to describe the self precisely in terms of being *in* the world as a self that is thrown or cast into situations in which engagement and commitment

---

[11]Ricoeur, *Husserl: An Analysis*, 12.

are unavoidable, and where authentic decisions must be made in the face of inevitable anxiety and death.[12]

While the importance of decisive choice on the part of the creature is emphasized in Scripture, making existentialist analysis a valuable tool in understanding the role of the will and the exercise of responsibility in crucial moments of decision, the contributions of Heidegger have to be weighed against his indebtedness to the Kantian tradition of the autonomous self. Heidegger attempts to describe the human situation entirely apart from divine revelation (he gave up his early call to the priesthood and, in the intellectual spirit of the day, adopted an atheistic hermeneutics). What makes Heidegger distinctive among modern existentialists is his deep preoccupation with Being as the basis of the existential choices human beings must make. He repudiates Husserl's separation of consciousness from the temporal world and emphasizes human involvement in the realm of Being. Because he is attempting as a non-Christian to describe the total setting of reality, he construes Being not as God but as that indefinable ground out of which the individual arises as possibility and not as mere actuality. He is first and foremost an ontologist who is concerned to restore the Being of beings.

There is something almost pantheistic about Heidegger's identification of Being and the self. The latter he designates *Dasein*, "being there."[13] The meaning of Being can be explored only from the context of the autonomous self, *Dasein*, who must in turn be seen in respect of the horizons of time. *Dasein* as conscious thinking ego must penetrate back through past time and repudiate every tradition that binds the self, including (for the Westerner) Platonism and Christianity. One must penetrate

---

[12]Heidegger's major earlier work is *Being and Time* (Oxford: Blackwell, 1962). For analysis, see Richard E. Palmer, *Hermeneutics: Interpretation Theory in Schleiermacher, Dilthey, Heidegger, and Gadamer* (Evanston: Northwestern University Press, 1969); George Alfred Schrader, Jr., ed., *Existential Philosophers: Kierkegaard to Merleau-Ponty* (New York: McGraw-Hill, 1967); Anthony C. Thistleton, *The Two Horizons: New Testament Hermeneutics and Philosophical Description* (Grand Rapids: Eerdmans, 1980).

[13]Heidegger, *Being and Time*, p. 62.

beyond even the more modern and narrow subjectivism of Kant, back to primordial Being where *Dasein* arises out of forgetfulness and hiddenness to the truth, in light of which the self is empowered to move forward into the future time of possibility with authenticity.

Heidegger's hermeneutical program will strike the Christian as a naturalism that tries to avoid the atomism of subjectivity by casting it into the larger setting of Being. Being seems, at least conceptually, to be firmly under the control of and even identified with emerging *Dasein*. The opening into Heidegger's hermeneutical circle is carefully guarded by the autonomous self. This door cannot be assaulted by theoretical science or deterministic methodologies, though they have their respective and relative legitimate functions. *Dasein* is prior and more primordial; it is immersed in a world in which there are no absolutes, no one pattern of truth or meaning, but only human projects that the reflective self must trace back beyond Western conceptual traditions to the preconceptual and precognitive level of primordial Being. God's self-revelation in nature, the self, and Scripture plays no role in any of this. *Dasein* explores the world in totally human terms.

Accordingly, Heidegger goes further than Kant in positing the autonomous self as center of the quest for meaning and understanding. While he deconstructs Kant's particular formulation of the critical enterprise, he reconstructs the latter by locating Being primordially in the nondiscursive moods and feelings of the self (e.g., the self-disclosures of fear, care, dread, anxiety, the sense of possibility and potentiality, the positing of meaning arising out of the self as it moves within its hermeneutical circle). He also speaks of the discourse of the self as it communicates with other persons (*Mitdasein*). In this, however, there is danger of losing oneself in the crowd and falling into authenticity. It is particularly in dread (*Angst*) and fear (*Furcht*) in the fact of death that Heidegger posits *Dasein's* authentic existence. Care (*Sorge*) brings the self back from mindless absorption in the mass of "they" and restores an authentic existentialist posture that reaches into the not-yet through personal freedom and decision.[14]

According to Heidegger, truth lies in the primordial freedom of the self, not in specific judgments or propositions. Enlightenment hermeneutics, personified by the Kantian autonomous self, is taken to its limit in the "standing-open" of Heidegger's *Dasein* and its repudiation of any objective, absolute truth. Authoritative Scripture is discarded, along with all other propositional absolutes. While *Dasein* is relative, historical, and in process of change, it is ultimately the only source of truth Heidegger allows. Self-understanding in light of one's possibilities and limitations in Being-towards-death is the hermeneutical norm. While conscience calls the self to authentic decision, it also arises out of *Dasein's* own primordially silent, subjective, and mystical sense of the "unarticulated uncanny" before an open and time-laden future. At this level of precognition there is no distinction between subject and object, no assertion, no articulated sense of truth or untruth, right or wrong.

As a hermeneutical method for biblical interpretation the Heideggerian program is so individualistic that it reduces to very subjective, though sometimes ingenious and insightful, interpretations when applied to specific biblical texts. With their manysided (polyvalent) interpretations of Jesus' parables, the writings of Ernst Fuchs, Robert Funk, and Dominic Crossan (see below) evidence a Heideggerian influence. The school of polyvalence holds that no objective interpretation of a parable is or can be given. Jesus does not invest the parables with enduring and infallible meaning; rather, each individual *Dasein* determines the scope and meaning of the text in an open-ended and autonomous search to become itself.

In his later writings,[15] Heidegger gives greater emphasis to

---

[14]Ibid., 225–35.

[15]Martin Heidegger, *An Introduction to Metaphysics* (New Haven: Yale University Press, 1959); idem, *On the Way to Language* (New York: Harper & Row, 1971); idem, *Poetry, Language, and Thought* (New York: Harper & Row, 1971). For Heidegger's affinities with Asian thought, see *Heidegger and Asian Thought*, Graham Parkes, ed. (Honolulu: University of Hawaii Press, 1988).

listening to Being (ontology) by way of primordial art and poetry and thus somewhat softens the theme of existential choice. Yet the priority of the autonomous *I* remains uppermost. There is therefore no substantial difference between the earlier and the later Heidegger; in all his writings he affirms the autonomy of the primordial experience of the self with its setting in pristine Being. This hermeneutical theme occupies pride of place over discursive language, subject-object distinctions, and notions of objective truth. Language is not essentially a tool or a means of giving information and communicating concepts but is the call of Being through the primordial poetry and art of "language-event." In a mystical and almost magical (and pantheistic) manner, Being as impersonal logos speaks and calls and collects humanity in primal gathering, much as a great painting gathers its parts into one integrated whole. *Dasein*, the self, is midwife of this gathering as it listens contemplatively, openly, receptively and yieldingly to the many-sided, polyvalent meanings of primal Being. One may observe that here Heidegger is not far from Zen Buddhism, with his appeal for the deconstruction of cognitive language and the return to some nondiscursive level of noncognitive "language," though his ontology of Being is problematic for Buddhism and its rejection of Being.[16]

The key to Heidegger's hermeneutical program, therefore, as for Bultmann and his successors in the school of the New Hermeneutic, is the priority of the experiencing self in determining truth. Truth is what is true "for me" as I hear and respond to the nonpropositional language of Being. Indeed, *Dasein* is the autonomous ego, which spins out the whole hermeneutical worldview about Being. The Kantian pole of subjective autonomy is therefore the beginning and the end of meaning and understanding in Heidegger's hermeneutical circle. There is no God and no objective revelation of God's interpretation of reality in nature or infallible Scripture. *Dasein* is thus thrown back on itself as the final source and arbiter of truth. It must be said, however, that recognizing these serious

---

[16]See Thistleton, *Two Horizons*, 34–42.

limitations, Heidegger's phenomenological analysis of anxiety, fear, care, and death affords valuable insight for the exegete in the exploration of the dark side of being-in-the-world-without-God.

Kerygmatic Existentialism: Rudolf Bultmann (1884–1976). Perhaps no contemporary interpreter has more deeply influenced New Testament hermeneutics and exegetical method than Heidegger's colleague at Marburg, Rudolf Bultmann. Adopting Heidegger's emphasis on *Dasein's* subjective experience and existentialist choice, he conceived of New Testament theology as anthropology and pursued a neo-Gnostic, antisupernaturalist interpretation of the biblical texts. A number of streams coalesce in Bultmann's thinking, most of them traceable to Kantian hermeneutics. From theological liberalism Bultmann gained the conviction, mainly through the influence of his teacher Wilhelm Herrmann, that faith is based not on belief in the doctrines or historical certainties of orthodox Christianity but on one's subjective religious experience. Faith is therefore freedom from all objective systems of thought, including inspired and authoritative Scripture. Authority resides, then, in the subjective pole of religious experience within the context of a thoroughly modernized Lutheranism, which had itself become deeply influenced by the dualism of neo-Kantianism. Herrmann, who had been influenced by Ritschl, accentuated the Kantian pole of subjectivity over against the pole of objective fact, the latter being construed in neo-Lutheran fashion as "works versus faith." Bultmann radically reinterpreted the Pauline "by faith alone" principle to mean that all earthly security must be abandoned, including the certainty of infallible Scripture, historical facts (except the fact that Jesus lived), and all traditional Christian theology. Even Herrmann's pietistic belief in the inner life of Jesus had to be discarded as a "work." Everything in the sphere of the Kantian pole of reason/science/history, insofar as it touched on biblical faith, had to be put to the flame by radical criticism in order to remove every external support; faith could not be based on anything objective or given.

As an exegete interpreting biblical texts, Bultmann did not

dismiss the pole of rationalistic determinism that operates within the scientific mode. Indeed, he accepted that form of inquiry as characteristic of the modern preunderstanding that must be respected by any responsible scholar unwilling to make a sacrifice of the intellect. Bultmann himself used deterministic historicism to deconstruct the New Testament documents in order to demonstrate their evolutionary emergence in the Hellenistic world of comparative philosophies and religions. His world is thoroughly dualistic and Kantian: genuine faith can be expressed only in the sphere of personal freedom where the primal word of God addresses the self directly, with no necessary point of contact in the public sphere that is dominated by objective facts, science, historical study, law, literature, and other human works, for all are subject to relativity and change. Bultmann's hermeneutical program is even more radical than Kant's, however. Kant's practical reason and ethical categorical imperative constituted a system of works and human security to which Bultmann would not give pride of place over the primordial voice of God that speaks to the self in existential encounter.

Hence the New Testament needs to be radically demythologized by surgical criticism in order to strip away the form of its Hellenistic mythology and reveal the existential moment of decision as of singular significance. In his *History of the Synoptic Tradition* and *Jesus and the Word*[17] he discloses his penchant for radical deconstruction of the biblical text at the deterministic pole of historical criticism. In his *Theology of the New Testament*[18] he lays out in detail his reinterpretation of a critically reassessed New Testament in existentialist terms that lie at the pole of personal freedom, as the self responds in faith to divine grace. Once radical criticism has done its job of deconstructing every touchpoint of security at the objective pole of historical fact (interpreted as "works" in Bultmann's Kantian neo-Lutheranism), the primal kerygma of the New

[17]Rudolf Bultmann, *The History of the Synoptic Tradition* (Oxford: Blackwell, 1963); idem, *Jesus and the Word* (London: Collins, 1958).

[18]Rudolf Bultmann, *Theology of the New Testament*, 2 vols. (London: SCM, 1952, 1955).

Testament can address the self with a call to authentic existence, in much the same way that Heidegger's Being addresses *Dasein* through a primordial and preconceptual call to authenticity.

Dialectical neoorthodox theology also plays a significant role in Bultmann's complex program of demythologizing. While it is true that in practice he reduces theology to anthropology, with its focus on the self, his avowed intention is to protect God from all idolatrous objectification. Nothing at the pole of scientific and historical research is capable of bearing the disclosure of the wholly other God and therefore cannot threaten faith in any way. False theologies *about* God (and erroneous views that the Scriptures are inerrant) result when one objectifies and asserts propositional doctrinal statements. God addresses the self directly, but not the self as object, for that would give the self mastery over God by objectifying one's personal religious experiences. It is only the self as subjective and existential, "on the way" and in continual conflict with an opposing yet gracious God who in the event of each moment offers grace and demands obedient response in faith. Thus God is encountered nowhere else than in the concrete present of one's responsibility and decision making. This means that authentic exegesis of the text of Scripture occurs only when the exegete is clear about the possibilities of human existence. And so, ironically, theology becomes anthropology, for the only touchpoint (univocality) between God and the world is in the moment of personal human decision in response to the proclaimed Word.

Once God and the self have been technically deobjectified by Bultmann's neo-Lutheran, neoorthodox doctrine of the total otherness of God, the self in practical terms finally emerges as the central subject and object of theology. The question of God and the question of the self are identical, as Bultmann insists in *Jesus Christ and Mythology*.[19] By a hermeneutical *tour de force* Bultmann implies that the disclosure of the wholly other God is to be identified with the experience of the self in existential

[19]Rudolf Bultmann, *Jesus Christ and Mythology* (London: SCM, 1960), 53; see 52–55.

encounter. Since God is disclosed neither in nature nor in history (Bultmann labels claims to common revelation in nature and special revelation in biblical history as objectifying and therefore idolatrous), the only possible ground for authentic biblical exegesis is one's present self-understanding. Hence, now-subjectivity is the only real objectivity.

Since one's self-understanding is constantly in dialectical encounter with the speaking God, exegesis is continually in flux and can never be final. Here we see the similarity of Bultmann to Wilhelm Dilthey, R. G. Collingwood, and Friedrich Gogarten.[20] The idealist hermeneutics of these historians undertakes the imaginative reconstruction of the past in the present by the interpreter-historian, whose reflective effort brings new disclosures to the self, and is a never-ending task of reinterpretation. An existentialist hermeneutics steers historical interpretation toward the possibilities of the future and is guided by the historian's own self-understanding as one who is "on the way."[21]

Thus it can be seen how alike are Bultmann's program and Kant's dualism, with their scientific and deterministic nature pole, which is concerned with fact, and their freedom pole, which is religious, practical, subjective, and concerned with value. Bultmann's exegesis of biblical texts is therefore radically dualistic. On the one hand he works from the deterministic pole to deconstruct the objective supernatural claims of Scripture in the realm of nature/history; on the other hand he reinterprets the denatured myths of the New Testament from the freedom pole in light of his own present "historic" self-understanding. Nature and objective history (respectively, *Natur* and *Historie*) comprise the realm of scientific factual knowledge. These are

---

[20]On Dilthey, see above, pp. 58–61; R. G. Collingwood, *The Idea of History* (Oxford: Clarendon, 1961); Friedrich Gogarten, *Demythologizing and History* (London: SCM, 1955).

[21]For extensive discussion of the role of existentialism in Bultmann's hermeneutical program, see John Macquarrie, *An Existentialist Theology: A Comparison of Heidegger and Bultmann* (London: SCM, 1955); idem, *The Scope of Demythologizing: Bultmann and His Critics* (London: SCM, 1960); and more critically, A. C. Thiselton, *Two Horizons*.

opposed by history in the new sense of "existential history" (*Geschichte*), which is history for faith alone as one faces new possibilities for self-understanding through personal decision.

We detect here a problem that has been endemic in Continental idealism from its inception. It is the final positioning of reality in the ideas and experience of the human ego and the consequent reduction of the texts of Scripture in biblical exegetical circles to two quite unrelated and unintegrated spheres and methodologies. One is a positivistic interpretation of the data by purely naturalistic and deterministic criteria that rule out the supernatural and the distinctively scriptural claims to objective authority. The other is an arbitrary subjectivism that locates history not in the past but in the present moment, as *Dasein* shapes its destiny by personal decision in the ever-recurring moments of freedom. At the Kantian value pole of personal freedom, Bultmann may be seen to be arbitrarily selecting what he feels are the primary "historic" (i.e., repeatable) themes from the New Testament; at the fact pole he may be seen to be arbitrarily rejecting what he deems to be the secondary historical, falsely objective and mythological themes of the texts. On both counts and at both poles the autonomous self controls the choices. Scripture speaks only where it is allowed to speak to the self-governing subjectivity of the ego, with its need to find meaning and possibility in the existential moment.

Crucial to Bultmann's hermeneutical program of denaturing the objective supernatural-redemptive themes of Scripture is his method of demythologizing. Myth is understood in neo-Kantian terms, especially through the eyes of Ernst Cassirer and Hans Jonas, along with Heidegger. Cassirer's *Language and Myth* and Jonas's *Gnosis und spätantiker Geist*[22] define the mythical as the uncritical objectification of immediate existential experience. Therefore the primitive conceptuality of the biblical world needs translation into the maturer thought of the

[22]Ernst Cassirer, *Language and Myth* (New York: Harper, 1946); Hans Jonas, *Gnosis und spätantiker Geist: II, 1, von der Mythologie zur mystischen Philosophie* (Goettingen: Vandenhoeck und Ruprecht, 1954).

contemporary scientific world. Since myth for Bultmann must be deobjectified because it has no objective validity as it stands (thus inerrant Scripture, miracles, substitutionary atonement, resurrection, and eschatology are not objective historical facts), the inner content and subjective truth of myth must be released by a process of demythologizing. Thereby the self gains a new (gnostic) understanding of its existential relation to transcendent power in the present.[23]

Accordingly, Bultmann does not himself believe that he is rejecting the deep meaning of Scripture or the one myth that cannot be demythologized, namely, the Christ-event itself, but only its obsolete worldview and an orthodox system of theology that no thinking modern person can accept without a sacrifice of the intellect. It is not his intention to make Christianity easy for modernity along the lines of the older liberalism but to confront the modern person with the heart of the kerygma in its call to decision, in view of God's radical love in the hiddenness of the present. This program calls for demythologizing, which Bultmann believes the New Testament itself invites as it exhorts the individual to find self-understanding in existential decision. The total destruction of every false security, purportedly along the lines of Paul's and Luther's principle of justification by faith alone, apart from works of the law, identifies the radical reduction that informs Bultmann's exegesis.

While Bultmann has provided many helpful insights by interpreting New Testament terminology through existential self-understanding, especially Paul's anthropology (his discussion of Pauline theology is the more imaginative and useful section of his *New Testament Theology*), it is nevertheless the case that Bultmann's existentialist hermeneutics transforms the message of the New Testament into another gospel. All the claims of Scripture that God has acted decisively and objectively in history are discarded as idolatrous objectifications of God and must be demythologized away from the objective pole of

---

[23]See Bultmann, *Jesus Christ and Mythology*, for a clear and concise presentation of his radical demythologizing.

nature/history to the subjective pole of personal, existential self-understanding. The virginal conception in human flesh of the preexistent Son, his perfect life as the God-man, the shedding of his blood on the cross in vicarious atonement that juridically propitiates divine wrath against sinners and graciously provides for their redemption, his resurrection from the dead, his ascension, and his future return to consummate on a cosmic scale his inaugurated reign, are all reductionistically explained away as primitive patterns of thought borrowed from Hellenistic mystery religions and Gnosticism. As such they require reinterpretation through nonobjective language that describes the meaning of Christ "for me" in light of my own personal existential possibilities, without any security outside my subjective faith in God's love.

Several observations may be made in critique of this deconstruction of classical biblical Christianity and its reconstruction along the lines of neo-Kantian, liberal Lutheran, and Heideggerian existentialist hermeneutics. The first, which will be explored in more detail in part 2 of our study, emphasizes the public nature of biblical claims in the objective arena of history. In order for personal experience to have any valid content it must arise from belief that the world is objectively this way or that, otherwise one's attitudes reduce to mere subjective idealism and solipsism. This was Husserl's problem. Bultmann does in fact adopt a specific worldview, but one that is more characteristic of nineteenth-century scientific belief: sensory experience in the phenomenal world is to be explained without remainder according to the category of deterministic causality (Kant's objective pole of nature, which is systematically interpreted by the organizing categories of the rational mind). Bultmann's objectivizing of the world according to modern naturalism prevents him from accepting what the New Testament claims is God's true and objective interpretation of the world in the public arena of proclamation. If Bultmann is at all influenced by twentieth-century revolutions in scientific thought (the perplexing theories of relativity, indeterminacy, and complementarity), they do not encourage him to allow any place for a supernatural objective revelation in history. They seem only to reinforce his claim that faith cannot be made to rest on the vagaries and fluctuations of human interpretation in the world of nature and history.

Why then does he insist on retaining the one remaining "myth," the Christ-kerygma, rather than translating it along the lines of older liberal theology, or even atheism? Karl Jaspers[24] took Bultmann to task for this apparent inconsistency and for not following through on his program. Jean-Paul Sartre, on the other hand, with his atheistic interpretation of Heidegger[25] would have suggested that Bultmann was holding sentimentally onto some mythical vestige of his neo-Lutheran pietism. If this were discarded, Bultmann would be able to go all the way with his program of demythologizing and reconstruct mythological theology totally as anthropology. All objective religious terms such as "God," "Christ," and "kerygma" would then be interpreted without remainder as possibilities of personal existence. If justification by faith were indeed anchored in absolutely no objective grounds whatever, then all mythical vestiges (such as the word "justification" itself) would require translation into purely naturalistic terms.

Were one to embark on the project of deconstructing all objective God-language, as Bultmann has done, consistency would require that all theological claims to objectivity be translated entirely in human terms. There then should be no vestiges of God-language remaining, since God could not be objectified in human thought. If God truly exists, he could not disclose himself as object, but must be experienced at the subjective pole of existential possibility. The final question, then, is to ask what Bultmann was really experiencing in the subjective, nonobjective moment of pure faith. What was the content, other than subjective and sentimental states of consciousness? Kant's attempt to construct a world of ideas objectively and universally true now seems to dead-end in the

---

[24]Karl Jaspers and Rudolf Bultmann, *Myth and Christianity* (New York: Farrar, Straus, 1958). For Jaspers, one myth can be translated only into another myth, not into the nonmyth of Bultmann's anthropology.

[25]Jean-Paul Sartre, *Being and Nothingness* (New York: Philosophical Library, 1956).

subjective idealism and solipsism of the existential moment of the ego.

While at selected points there may be aids to understanding the New Testament in Bultmann's Heideggerian, neo-Kantian neo-Lutheranism (we have mentioned his existentialist analysis of Pauline theology—an analysis that contains valuable insights), his hermeneutical method as a whole lacks credibility because it is not sufficiently objective to allow the phenomena of the New Testament to speak on their own terms. All that is left of the original kerygma and its historical objectivity is a wholly naturalistic historicism at the "fact" pole of literary/historical criticism, and a neo-Kantian pietism at the value pole of existential subjectivity. The self in its subjectivity, wrapped in the language of traditional piety that no longer has any substantial denotative content, is all that is left. Hence as a historian and as a pietist, Bultmann offers unreliable exegesis. It is not genuinely phenomenological because it does not accurately describe the phenomena of biblical faith.

The Fusion of Horizons: Gadamer and the New Hermeneutic. Bultmann's appropriation of Heidegger's existentialism was imaginative and even at times brilliant, but it centered on the crisis decisions of the self and therefore tended to be solitary and subjective. Appreciative of Bultmann's work, and building on what he considered his lasting contribution to the hermeneutical quest for meaning and understanding, Hans-Georg Gadamer nonetheless felt constrained to return to Heidegger, the principal source of Bultmann's hermeneutics. In *Truth and Method*, his major work,[26] Gadamer tries to locate meaning in the larger context of community. The horizon of the conscious self is addressed by, listens to, and finally fuses with the ontological disclosure of being, much as one is spoken to by a work of art, is drawn into its presuppositions and is compelled to play its "game" on the ground of its own canvas. The canvas is larger than the person who beholds it, just as experience is larger than the subjective self who interprets it.[27]

---

[26]Hans-Georg Gadamer, *Truth and Method* (New York: Seabury, 1975).
[27]Ibid., 39–95.

Accordingly, Gadamer's hermeneutical method appears at first glance to be less existentialist ("for me") than phenomenological ("within the world"). This means that one who interprets the past (e.g., an exegete interpreting Scripture) should not attempt simply to recapture the past existentially for what it means "to me" at the subjective pole, nor simply deal with the details of the historical canvas as neutral items at the objective factual pole, but recognize the larger communal context of the past as it represents itself in the present, and stand within it.

Gadamer is describing what has come to be known as the New Hermeneutic, the attempt to get beyond the dualism of Descartes and Kant and fuse the horizon of the self with the horizon of the larger canvas of past experience as it invites one to stand within it in the present. What occurs, he argues, when the interpreter stands within the larger work of art and listens to it speaking, while retaining one's own horizon of concepts, is "language-event" or "speech-happening." In this event the past is not simply replicated as past but gives occasion to a new disclosure of being through the fusion of the self with the piece of art (say, a portion of Scripture, such as a parable). Gerhard Ebeling, Ernst Fuchs, Robert Funk, and J. Dominic Crossan[28] are representative of those who have articulated the New Hermeneutic in the spirit of Gadamer and Heidegger and have interpreted hermeneutics as ontological language-event through the disclosure of story and art form.

This philosophical/aesthetic program sounds attractive and offers much of value to the evangelical interpreter of Scripture, especially when it is recognized that what goes on in the believer's experience in reading Scripture is like being spoken to by something (or someone) larger through the medium of story and imagined picture. The problem with Gadamer's hermeneutical method is that it remains essentially

---

[28]Gerhard Ebeling, *Word and Faith* (London: SCM, 1963); Ernst Fuchs, *Studies of the Historical Jesus* (London: SCM, 1964); Robert Funk, *Language, Hermeneutic, and Word of God. The Problem of Language in the New Testament and Contemporary Theology* (New York: Harper & Row, 1966); John Dominic Crossan, *In Parables: The Challenge of the Historical Jesus* (New York: Harper & Row, 1973).

Kantian, despite his disclaimers to the contrary. It does not allow the original speakers of the past (the inspired writers of Scripture or the historical Jesus of the Gospels) to posit objective propositional meaning that is binding on the present reader. Since hermeneutics is an aesthetic process that is constantly changing in new settings and in new fusions with the concepts of the interpreter, there can never be an eternal set of teachings, propositions, or objective meanings that come from the past into the present. Rather, the horizon of the past is continually opening itself to new interpretations and meanings in light of the present interpreter's experience. Thus the parables of Jesus, for example, are pregnant artistic expressions that invite polyvalent (manysided) meanings as the interpreter brings his or her own experience to bear upon the experience of Jesus. Jesus does not invest a parable with only one meaning but leaves each one open as an invitation to the hearer to let the possibilities inherent in the Word speak to him or her in changing situations. Indeed, Gadamer insists that the original speaker who speaks and the artist who creates is not the best interpreter of his or her own work.[29]

Thus while Gadamer tries to give due regard to the horizon of past historical experience, in actual fact he gives priority to the contemporary horizon of "being present" (*Dabeiseins*) in preaching or in the communal experience of art-form.[30] He has sketched with heavier pen the horizon of the interpreting self, for that is where the final authority lies. Gadamer and his school are not so much interested in discovering normative historical facts. Once again, like Heidegger (and Kant at his subjective pole of value, as well as Schleiermacher with his subjective hermeneutics of religion as art), Gadamer is interested primarily in what the language event of the art-form means "for me." Hence the school continues to be deeply committed to existentialism, and hermeneutics is again reduced to anthropology. Horizons are always changing; consequently the text or work of art never speaks to the

[29]Gadamer, *Truth and Method*, p. 130.
[30]Ibid.

interpreter as inspired and authoritative but is itself dependent for its meaning and significance on the disclosure of the moment and the questions put to it by the self. Thus the understanding of a biblical text, as of any other text, is a creative process of listening and asking questions that are never identical with the intention of the original speaker or author. Meaning and significance are never reproductive of the original setting and therefore never intrinsically authoritative.[31] A horizon is always on the move; it can never be objectified, but must be experienced as part of the processing life-world.

Not only does the New Hermeneutic extend to new horizons the older Kantian hermeneutics of the autonomous self, but in its attempt to get away from the charge of subjectivity by placing the self within the larger canvas of language-event, it apotheosizes the abstraction of "language speaking," which is also typical of Heidegger.[32] The terminology appears at first impressive, but since in the nature of the case only persons speak intelligible language (the heavens also declare the glory of God, but only because the personal God speaks commonly through nature), it is inappropriate to speak of "language speaking." It is a contribution of Anglo-American philosophies of language analysis (discussed in part 2) to point out that it is persons who speak and are listened to; either they are listened to as authoritative (e.g., when the authors of Scripture are taken to be normative) or else the self assumes the right to speak authoritatively in their stead. Language about "language speaking" and "word-event," however, simply veils the fact that in the New Hermeneutic, as in all the variations of Kantian hermeneutics, it is the autonomous ego that is actually doing the speaking as well as defining what is meaningful and significant "for oneself." In the "language-event" of hearing or reading, the hearer-reader in actuality substitutes the multiple meanings arising from the self for the intention of the original speaker or writer. While Gadamer aims to overcome subjectiv-

---

[31]Ibid., 147.

[32]See Heidegger, *On the Way to Language* (New York: Harper & Row, 1971), 85; cf. Gadamer, *Truth and Method*, 367.

ity by his notion of a fusion of horizons arising from the autonomy of the text and the autonomy of the self, the predominant horizon in his program remains that of the reader, whose perspective is dominated by the ego's own assessment of the existential possibilities of the "event."

There is an element of truth in the fusion of horizons theme, of course, which is intrinsic to the work of God in the world of natural revelation and in the special revelation of Scripture through the ministry of the Holy Spirit. What guards biblical faith from becoming mere feeling and subjectivity, however, is the claim of Scripture to be objective truth that is valid in any moment of history. The obedient reader and hearer of the Word will accordingly respond in faith to God's gracious invitation to repent, believe in the Son of God who brings salvation, pursue holiness, and proclaim the good news of salvation to a fallen world. The bridge between the salvific event of the first century, accurately attested by the believing witnesses to Christ, and the present moment of the experiencing self, is not the self but the Holy Spirit. Only the Spirit's work within the believer can bridge past and present and preserve the objective authority of the biblical witness. Without a strong doctrine of the Holy Spirit's interpretive ministry, hermeneutical authority defaults to the ego that fuses the past to its present on its own terms, thus creating the past in its own image.

French Structuralism. Another related but slightly different line of thought develops from Husserl's pursuit of the pure essences that arise out of human consciousness. In the Russian and French schools of structuralism (represented by V. Propp, A. J. Greimas, and Daniel Patte,[33] among others) the interpreter attempts to go beyond the historical or diachronic (through-time) elements of a text to the symbolic code that is structured

[33]V. Propp, *Morphology of the Folktale*, 2d ed., trans. L. A. Wagner (Austin: University of Texas Press, 1968); A. J. Greimas, *Structural Semantics: An Attempt at a Method* (Lincoln: University of Nebraska, 1984); Daniel Patte, "Narrative and Structure and the Good Samaritan," *Semeia 2* (Missoula: Scholars, 1974). See Tremper Longman III, *Literary Approaches*, 27–45, for an overview and critique of the school.

into it and that transcends or collapses all time frames into one transcendent time-frame in the present (the synchronic, or synchronized time). The interpreter must delve beneath surface meanings to the universally common structural patterns or "essences" that lie within a text and go beyond the author's own intention to deeper subconscious grids or genres of meaning embedded in language itself.

In the process of discovery, the reader is not passive in respect to the text but active and more than equally determinative in the production of its meaning. The original intent of the historical speaker or author does not figure large in the determination of textual meaning (authoritative Scripture is therefore discounted in biblical application), since objective noumenal facts are unattainable, as Kant insisted. Only the intuited phenomena of human consciousness are available for analysis. Therefore one must begin and conclude the structural analysis of a text with one's own conscious and subconscious interaction with it. Hence, like Gadamer's hermeneutics on another related track, multiple meanings of any given text will arise in the consciousness of the interpreter, depending on the contemporary context of the self, which is always in flux. The intention of the original speaker or author (e.g., Jesus or Paul) is bracketed, and preference is given to the identification of structural codes or genres that lie deep in the structure of language, as reflected in the text and in the subconsciousness of the interpreter. These structural codes come to consciousness when the self expresses its expectations of the text and thus sets up the semantic field of possible meanings.

All of this points back to Husserl's hermeneutical quest for transhistorical essences that lie deep in the human consciousness. The quest is typical of the hermeneutics of contemporary philosophical neo-Gnosticism. For Husserl, the gap between the self and structural essences is leapt over by sheer intuition of the pure phenomena deep within the consciousness. For structuralists it is a quest for generic global structures that lie at the subconscious level of language. Its analysis of language in categories of genre and generative poetics attempts to synchronize the diachronic (historical-cultural) range of meanings but aims at the suspension of any immediate single meaning in favor of a deeper pluralism of possible structural meanings. Since everything is language, the goal of the interpreter is not to isolate any particular message or to extract any single signification but to establish the generic structures of the text and allow its multiple blossoming of meanings. While the text is said to be autonomous, in actual fact the mind of the perceiving interpreter is indispensable in bringing forth the range of meanings possible in any given text. One does this by interacting with the text in a manner that resembles Gadamer's metaphorical fusion of horizons, with its imaginative interplay and generation of new significance within the interpreter's own context.

More recent structuralist theory has reacted against the charge of its critics that the school brackets out the category of diachronic history. The fact remains, however, that the major thrust of the school, whether its practitioners apply its hermeneutics primarily in literary or in social contexts, continues to be the identification of metahistorical or synchronic codes that are thought to be discernible within historical and cultural settings. The practical effect of structuralist hermeneutics is therefore often an imaginative pluralism of meanings, ultimately under the control of the interpreter's own perspectives and experiences. Structuralist successors to Kant interpret Scripture on the Kantian third level of aesthetic criticism, with all of the subjectivism entailed in that method. In spite of their claim that structuralist hermeneutics uncovers the deep and essential codes of language, their ostensible pursuit of objective codes more often than not masks the subjective grids of structure superimposed on any given text by the individual interpreter, thus generating and even encouraging multiple meanings as the desirable goal of hermeneutics.

This plurality of meaning is further accented by the hermeneutics of deconstruction associated with Jacques Derrida[34] (by way of Saussure). Derrida criticizes the language-event school as logocentric and deemphasizes speech in prefer-

[34]See *Derrida and Biblical Studies, Semeia 23* (Missoula: Scholars, 1982).

ence for the written word. Yet he attacks the relationship of author and intention, separating signifier and sign so that the very fabric of language itself is threatened by multiple meanings. In the world of deconstruction one is very far indeed from the authoritative intent of Jesus and the inspired writers of Scripture. J. Dominic Crossan, who relies heavily on Derrida's program of deconstruction, relativizes the biblical message and encourages polyvalent meanings in the parables of Jesus, and even in respect to the meaning of Jesus himself.[35] One "plays" with the text, since the speaker or author has given no authoritative, univocal meaning to it. Yet, interestingly, Derrida holds to the priority of human reason as he deconstructs the arguments of other schools and exposes their limits and blind spots (*aporias*). The failure of communication on the written level, not to mention speech itself, he attributes (as an atheist) to the absence of God (the "transcendental signified"). His Christian critic, Michael Edwards, appreciates Derrida's analysis of this slippage of language in the modern world, but attributes it to the Fall, which is a very different epistemology.[36] This illustrates again that philosophers who reject the Christian worldview may often have valuable insights to offer the biblical exegete on the shared ontological level of God's common revelation in nature and self, but not on the epistemological or theological level, where the self-revealing God of Scripture speaks authoritatively about the nature of reality and the state of the human heart.

Exploring the Realm of Symbols: The Phenomenology of Paul Ricoeur. In the writings of Ricoeur[37] one can see the fusion

---

[35] J. D. Crossan, *Cliffs of Fall: Paradox and Polyvalence in the Parables of Jesus* (New York: Seabury, 1980).

[36] Michael Edwards, *Toward a Christian Poetics* (London: Macmillan, 1984). See also Christopher Norris, *Derrida* (Cambridge: Harvard University Press, 1988) for a recent interpretation and critique of Derrida.

[37] Paul Ricoeur, *Fallible Man: Philosophy of the Will*, trans. Charles Kelbley (Chicago: Regnery, 1960); idem, *The Symbolism of Evil*, trans. Emerson Buchanan (Boston: Beacon Press, 1967); idem, *Husserl: An Analysis of His Phenomenology* (Evanston: Northwestern University Press, 1967); idem, *The Conflict of Interpretations: Essays in Hermeneutics* (Evanston: Northwestern University Press, 1974); idem, "Biblical Hermeneutics," in *Semeia IV* (Mis-

of Husserlian and Heideggerian phenomenology, Bultmannian existentialism, Gadamerian historiography, structuralist hermeneutics, with a central focus on metaphorical language. For Ricoeur it is in the "semantic event," where text and interpreter are fused together through the interplay of metaphor and symbol, that one experiences a "secondary naïveté," without giving up critical privilege. The objective sense of the text and the interpreter's response to it are lifted beyond objectivity and subjectivity to the level of ontological dialectic in which the world is disclosed in new ways to the self in changing situations. As contexts change, the text decontextualizes itself and distances itself from the original intention of the author or speaker, allowing a dynamic performance of mediation by language itself. Linguistics, genre, and structure do not function therefore as guarantors of objective meaning but are themselves part of the hermeneutical circle that draws itself around the text and the preunderstanding of the interpreter. Thus while it is claimed that the text has authority, it does not actually function as such in any objective or propositional sense, since the open-endedness of hermeneutics compels the interpreter to deconstruct the text of any claim to changeless original meaning and to reconstruct it within contemporary contexts that are continually subject to the dynamics of change.

While the grammatico-historical science of linguistics works within a closed system of a past language or culture (so OT Hebrew and Aramaic and NT Greek) and assists the discovery of what a text *meant* in that historical context, hermeneutics (it is argued) deals with the continual unfolding of what the text *means* in the open universe of signs.[38] This means

soula: Scholars, 1975), 29–145; idem, *The Rule of Metaphor* (Toronto: University of Toronto Press, 1977); idem, *Interpretation Theory* (Fort Worth: Texas Christian University Press, 1976); idem, *Essays on Biblical Interpretation* (Philadelphia: Fortress, 1980).

[38]Paul Ricoeur, "The Problem of Double Meaning as Hermeneutic and as Semantic Problem," in *The Conflict of Interpretations: Essays in Hermeneutics*, 62–78. This Kantian contrast between the science of discovering what a text meant and the subjective and ecclesial hermeneutics of what a text means in changing contexts is also articulated by Krister Stendahl, "Biblical Theology, Contempo-

that the original semantic signs of Scripture are not normative as the inspired and unchanging Word of God for all historical contexts. Ricoeur's hermeneutical method requires that the present meaning of a biblical text, as it exists for me existentially and for the church corporately in worship, is not tied referentially and objectively to its original historical context. There is no all-embracing hermeneutics of meaning. The fullness of language as it is mediated by religious symbols and myths requires the rejection of precise univocal (literal and objectively true) theology. The light of the emotions and ecclesial worship lead to deeper meanings revealed by these religious myths and symbols, which are ever changing as history and human experience flows onward.

Ricoeur warns that his focus on myth and symbol is not to be misconstrued as gnosis, for gnosis claims to be objective knowledge, while myth is naked symbol. Myth is not an explanation but an opening up and a disclosure of what otherwise would remain closed and hidden.[39] Thus Ricoeur works mainly out of the aesthetic value pole of Kantian dualism, reaching back, in his own words, into the prenarrative root of myth in the consciousness that is structured lower than any narration, fable, or legend.[40] Multiple narration, stories, myths, symbols, and theologies arise from this primordial structure of being. Hence, none is normative and once-for-all, and all require demythologizing at the scientific pole of rigorous, critical-historical method: "demythologization is the irreversible gain of truthfulness, intellectual honesty, objectivity."[41] On the other hand, modern hermeneutics seeks to make contact with the fundamental symbols of consciousness. Given its commitment to the autonomy of the critical ego, hermeneutics cannot go back to a primitive naïveté, for the immediacy of the original belief has been irremediably lost: "But if we can no longer live the great symbolism of the sacred in accordance with

---

rary," in *The Interpreter's Dictionary of the Bible* (New York: Abingdon Press, 1962), 418–32.

[39]Ricoeur, *The Symbolism of Evil*, 165.

[40]Ibid., 166.

[41]Ibid., 350.

the original belief in them, we can, we modern men, aim at a second naïveté in and through criticism. In short, it is by *interpreting* that we can *hear* again."[42]

Hence Ricoeur's hermeneutical program, brilliant at points in its analysis of human phenomena such as guilt and sin, nevertheless rejects the objective immediacy of a personal encounter with Christ shared univocally (i.e., on the same terms) with the earliest believers of the New Testament, since the primitive naïveté of evangelical faith is "irremediably lost"). In its place is a "second naïveté," a philosophical "contact with symbols."[43] Belief and criticism are held together dialectically as in Kantian dualism; the transcendental ego remains authoritative at both polarities. Like Bultmann, whom he cites favorably,[44] Ricoeur allows the presuppositions of the critical ego to demythologize the Scriptures of their claim to objective theological authority at the scientific pole, while holding on to nonbinding mythological religious symbols at the value pole.[45]

Ricoeur can be read with some profit if one is discerning of his larger commitment to a hermeneutical view that is inimical to historic biblical faith. Unlike his earlier mentor, Gabriel Marcel, whose phenomenology is, at least in this writer's eye, much more conducive to illuminating biblical themes, Ricoeur remains a thoroughgoing Kantian. His hermeneutical program, no less than Kant's, claims that the ego is authoritative in the description and diagnosis of reality. That is

---

[42]Ibid., 351. His emphasis. See also 352.

[43]Ibid., 353. For a brief critique of Ricoeur's concept of "second naïveté," see Royce G. Gruenler, *New Approaches to Jesus and the Gospels*(Grand Rapids: Baker, 1982), 146.

[44]Ricoeur, *The Symbolism of Evil*, 350–53.

[45]Ibid., 352. For a more sympathetic reading of Ricoeur's hermeneutics for evangelical thought, see Kevin J. Vanhoozer, "The Semantics of Biblical Literature: Truth and Scripture's Diverse Literary Forms," in D. A. Carson and John D. Woodbridge, eds., *Hermeneutics, Authority, and Canon* (Grand Rapids, Zondervan, 1986), 81, 90. See also David C. Steinmetz, "The Superiority of Pre-Critical Exegesis," *Theology Today* 37 (1980): 27–38; A. C. Thiselton, *Two Horizons*, 120–21; Moisés Silva, on Ricoeur, Origen, and the allegorical method, *Has the Church Misread the Bible?* (Grand Rapids: Zondervan, 1987, 57–75.

to say, at the end of "play" as at the beginning of "play" (for that is what the open-ended game of hermeneutics is all about, according to Ricoeur), it is in fact the autonomous self who controls the rules of the game.[46]

Neo-Hegelianism and Marxist Political Theology: The Hermeneutics of Praxis in Pannenberg, Moltmann, and Liberation Circles. In *Jesus—God and Man*,[47] (1960), Wolfhart Pannenberg reacted against the tendency of German idealism to separate theology from history. He made his starting point the history of Jesus' life, death, and resurrection, working upward rather than downward from the kerygma like Bultmann, or from the Trinity, like Barth. He shifted his focus from the value pole of religious subjectivity to the fact pole of history, locating Jesus' resurrection solidly in history instead of in the realm of existential faith.[48] In his writings he criticizes the positivism and cultural relativism of Troeltsch and his successors—views that rule out the possibility of God's supernatural acts in the historical arena. For Troeltsch, the absolutely unique does not occur in history; hence all historical data must be interpreted on analogy of repeatable experience. Pannenberg attempts to demonstrate the prejudice of this hermeneutical presupposition, which would eliminate all novelty and creativity from history and would effectively disallow God from acting and speaking objectively in the world of time and space.

Pannenberg places his finger on a fundamental hermeneutical presupposition governing much contemporary liberal exegesis and theology: God neither reveals himself nor is experienced at the fact pole of historical and scientific inquiry because that area is governed by the category of natural causality, dictated by the rational mind. God can be experienced

---

[46]This is further illustrated in Ricoeur's virtual rejection of biblical eschatology in favor of fictional, ideological symbolism, which he feels may afford utopian evocations for a new order. See his 1975 lectures at the University of Chicago, *Lectures on Ideology and Utopia*, ed. George H. Taylor (New York: Columbia University Press, 1987).

[47]Wolfhart Pannenberg, *Jesus—God and Man* (London: SCM, 1968).

[48]Ibid., 109. See also his *Basic Questions in Theology*, 3 vols. (London: SCM, 1970, 1971, 1973) 1:15–80; A. Thiselton, *Two Horizons*, 74–84.

only at the value pole of nonobjective religious experience—so the Kantian model.

But in resisting Kantian dualism, at least to the extent of opening up the fact pole to such unique events as the resurrection of Jesus, Pannenberg nevertheless insists that the history of biblical faith is not to be understood as special salvation-history, but belongs rather to the nature of universal history itself, much as Hegel had argued a century earlier. In rejecting Dilthey's and Troeltsch's relativism he needs an absolute in order to succeed in the attack. Although he does not rely on objective inerrant Scripture (a hermeneutical view he rejects), he nevertheless selects from the biblical tradition one unifying theme that he believes encompasses the universal whole: the eschatological event of Jesus Christ which anticipates the end of history in the midst of history, and thereby opens up the future for us. While this view differs somewhat from Hegel's pantheism, it is nevertheless Hegelian in that both agree that the truth of the whole will be visible only at the end of history.[49]

Pannenberg stands with Hegel in insisting that the present dynamic process of history, though appearing at the present to be unrelated, relative, and contradictory, is a rational whole whose unity will be revealed only at the end. Pannenberg's major quarrel with Hegel is that the latter claims to know too much about the end through rational reflection, while he himself believes that one must walk by faith on the ground of what Jesus Christ has done in his death and resurrection at the mid-point of history, the central event that inaugurates the end.[50] Pannenberg nevertheless stands within the Kantian hermeneutical circle. This is clear from his adaptation of Hegel's process philosophy of universal history and from his insistence that although the value pole of theology must inform the fact pole of scientific research (thus loosening up Troeltsch's positivism and Bultmann's dualism), scholarly interpretation of

---

[49]Pannenberg acknowledges his debt to Hegel in *Basic Questions in Theology*, 2:22.

[50]Ibid.

biblical data is still subject to the relativities of history, so that traditional phrases in Scripture no longer carry their original meaning in the changed situation of the present.

Pannenberg has therefore made only a token attempt to rescue history from relativity, since the death and resurrection of Jesus Christ no longer mean what they did to the early church. The horizon of Scripture must be fused with the thought-forms of the present, a view Pannenberg shares with Gadamer.[51] The death-resurrection motif is therefore only an eschatological hope that at the end of history conflicting views over meaning and significance will somehow find final resolution. Meanwhile, the autonomous horizon of the interpreter continues to control the significance of data at both the value pole and the fact pole. This essentially Kantian hermeneutical outlook opens the way to interpret Scripture under the pressure of present agendas, among which are political programs with distinctive political theologies of neo-Hegelian and Marxist character. These become part of the process of a universal world history that moves inexorably into the eschatological future.

This political theme is picked up by Jürgen Moltmann, who shares the fusion of horizons hermeneutics with Gadamer and Pannenberg. Fusing Barthian neoorthodox theology with a Marxist-existentialist hermeneutics of hope stemming from the atheistic philosopher Ernst Bloch (1885–1977), Moltmann interprets the process of history as a continual step into the open future of possibility.[52] Like Pannenberg, Moltmann finds the hermeneutical core of the New Testament in the eschatological vision opened up by the resurrection of Jesus. When that eschatological perspective of the early church is recaptured, the contemporary Christian scholar can become a true critic of the past and of the misinterpretation of history by the Western church. The eschatological vision of the New Testament church was focused on the exploited poor; hence in our day there can be a fusion of that horizon with a Marxist analysis of

[51]Ibid., 1:96–136.

[52]Jürgen Moltmann, *Theology of Hope* (London: SCM, 1967); idem, *The Crucified God* (New York: Harper & Row, 1974); idem, *The Trinity and the Kingdom* (New York: Harper & Row, 1981).

contemporary exploitation, leading to biblically informed adaptations of modern socialist models for the alleviation of political and economic oppression.[53]

The political hermeneutics of the gospel has been of central concern not only to Moltmann,[54] it is now also at the forefront of Continental, American, and third-world exegesis and theology. It remains to be seen whether these advocates of idealistic neo-Hegelian and neo-Marxist hermeneutics can overcome the lack of exegetical data for radical revolutionary political praxis in the New Testament, or the well-attested failure of Marxist-derived models of socialism in the twentieth century.[55] It appears reasonably certain, however, that radical social political theories based on Continental Hegelian-Marxist idealism will continue to influence liberal biblical hermeneutics and exegesis into the foreseeable future, in spite of global evidence of the failure of liberalism and collectivism in the modern world.[56]

---

[53]Moltmann, *Theology of Hope*, 106.

[54]See Moltmann, "Towards a Political Hermeneutics of the Gospel," *Union Seminary Quarterly Review* 23 (1968): 303–23.

[55]For critical appraisals of socialist models in the twentieth century, see Paul Johnson, *Modern Times: The World from the Twenties to the Eighties* (New York: Harper & Row, 1984); Michael Polanyi, *Personal Knowledge* (New York: Harper & Row, 1964), 203–45.

[56]For examples of the literature of liberation hermeneutics, see Gustavo Gutiérrez, *A Theology of Liberation* (Maryknoll: Orbis Books, 1973); José Porfirio Miranda, *Marx and the Bible: A Critique of the Philosophy of Oppression* (Maryknoll: Orbis, 1974); José Miguez Bonino, *Revolutionary Theology Comes of Age* (London: SPCK, 1975); Elizabeth Schüssler Fiorenza, *In Memory of Her* (New York: Crossroad, 1983); Elsa Tamez, ed., *Through Her Eyes: Women's Theology from Latin America* (Maryknoll: Orbis Books, 1989); Marc Ellis and Otto Maduro, eds., *The Future of Liberation Theology: Essays in Honor of Gustavo Gutiérrez* (Maryknoll: Orbis Books, 1989). For a critique, see J. A. Kirk, *Liberation Theology: An Evangelical View from the Third World* (London: Marshall, Morgan and Scott, 1979). The global collapse of communism has discredited Marxist hermeneutics and is pressuring its advocates to adopt milder forms of socialism and ecology as focal issues.

4

EXEGETICAL APPLICATION: GABRIEL MARCEL ON CREATIVE FIDELITY AND DISPOSABILITY

Gabriel Marcel, a prominent Christian European philosopher of the existentialist school, is concerned to describe the phenomenon of the existing, thinking, and choosing self in relation to other selves. In so doing he discovers that region where the personal "I" stands in creative fidelity and disposability, or servanthood, to other persons. Marcel notes that a number of fresh ways of looking at Jesus emerge from such a study and dissipate the staleness of ordinary analysis of the gospel texts. A fundamental phenomenon of human existence is the inescapability of incarnate being, not only in respect of my own personal experience where I and my body are inseparable, but also for my relationship with others and they with me in copresence. Indeed, for Marcel *esse est co-esse*, "to be is to be together," in incarnate and proximate relationship to one another, revealing myself to them and being revealed to in turn. Personal existence is charged with significance because of mutual self-revelation to others: When I assert that I exist I mean to imply more than that I am only for myself; I am manifesting myself to others. The prefix *ex* in the word *exist* conveys a centrifugal or outward movement toward the external world: "I exist; that means I have something by which I can be known or identified: 'There is my body.' "[1]

[1]Gabriel Marcel, *Creative Fidelity*, ed. and trans. Robert Rosenthal (New York: Noonday, 1964), 17.

If we think of Jesus in this sense, the Marcellian themes of centrifugal revelation clarify Jesus' self-disclosure and incarnate hospitality by which he invites his hearers to participate in a certain plenitude. Incarnate being, hospitality, disposability to others, and receptivity all describe the phenomenon who is Jesus: "Thus the ambiguous term 'receptivity' has a wide range of meaning extending from suffering or undergoing to the gift of self; for hospitality is a gift of one's own, i.e., of oneself."[2]

As incarnate "I" Jesus "takes upon himself" and "opens himself to" participation through the language of good faith as opposed to bad faith. Incarnate in his words and acts, Jesus is present to the interpreter as "thou" and addresses him or her in the second person. Marcel is concerned to reinstate the priority of the first- and second-person personal pronouns against the distant third-person personal pronouns *him*, *her*, or *it*. Jesus evidences his presence by giving priority to the personal pronoun *I* and to the pronouns *thou*, *you*, and *we* in his address. The gospel interpreter is therefore encouraged to focus more on the presence-language of Jesus (I, thou, we), and not exclusively on an analysis of "he" and "him" (third person). The latter occurs when Jesus becomes primarily the object of distant critical analysis that does not permit him to address the hearer or reader on the personal level of "I am" and "do thou likewise."

The evangelists portray Jesus by reporting his ordinary address and response. Marcel writes, "I address the second person when what I address can respond in some way—and that response cannot be translated into words. The purest form of invocation—prayer—embodied imperfectly in the uttered word, is a certain kind of inner transfiguration, a mysterious influx, and ineffable peace."[3] But the distant analysis of another can destroy the uniqueness of "I," "thou," and the unity of "we": "When I consider another individual as *him*, I treat him as essentially absent. . . ."[4]

[2]Ibid., 28.
[3]Ibid., 32.
[4]Ibid.

There is, however, a presence that is really an absence. Sometimes we act toward somebody who is present as though he or she were absent. For instance, if I merely talk about the weather with someone or gather biographical bits of information from him as though he were filling out a questionnaire, I treat him as essentially absent. Or if someone asks me similar questions, I too become a third person and am no longer "I" or "thou," but only a pen that traces words on paper. The real meaning of persons comes about when there is a bond of feeling between the "I" and the "thou," and "a unity is established in which the other person and myself become *we*, and this means that he ceases to be *him* and becomes *thou*. . . ."[5] When the other person ceases to be a mere object of conversation and is allowed to address me personally, we coalesce and fuse into a living unity of mutual openness: "The path leading from dialectic to love has now been opened."[6]

The biblical interpreter who follows Marcel's model will first set out to describe Jesus' use of the first and second personal pronouns "I," "thou," and "you," and the response of those with whom he shares the joy of the new age that is breaking in. Those who hear and see him but keep him in the distant third person treat him as though he were filling out a questionnaire and were essentially absent. Accordingly, a sympathetic interpretation of the Gospels would encourage the interpreter to be open to the presence of Jesus, not only as he speaks to his historical audience but as he addresses the critic himself. This is perhaps the hardest demand of Marcel's hermeneutical method; but as applied to gospel interpretation it is the only way of getting around the falsification that comes from objectifying Jesus as a mere "him" to be analyzed neutrally from outside without personal confrontation. There would appear to be no neutral ground, however. Marcel's hermeneutics of persons-in-relation requires that the gospel interpreter be open to the presence of Jesus who continues to be incarnate in his words and acts. When one allows himself to be confronted by the incarnate

[5]Ibid., 33.

[6]Ibid.

Jesus who speaks and acts, unity is established in which Jesus ceases to be a mere "him" and becomes the addressing "thou." The reader is then translated from a distant dialectic to a dialogue of openness:

> The being whom I love can hardly be a third person for me at all; yet he allows me to discover myself; my outer defenses fall at the same time as the walls separating me from the other person fall. He moves more and more into the circle with reference to which and outside of which there exist third persons who are the "others."[7]

Marcel maintains that only when we so communicate with other persons do we truly communicate with ourselves and experience transformation through inward relaxation and escape retraction into ourselves that mutilates relationships. In gospel exegesis, an openness to Jesus as incarnate "thou" opens up a region of fruitful relationships that transcend the closed system of objectification and abdication characteristic of traditional criticism. It is "a kind of vital milieu for the soul."[8] In an attitude of openness I expose myself to Jesus' claims and his gracious invitation, instead of protecting myself from him by using closed third-person language. If I detach myself from his invitation to relationship and insist on examining him from outside by a methodology of doubt, the relationship is fractured. A decisive conversion in outlook is required for the interpreter to enter into hermeneutical communion. It asks that the critic relinquish his demand to control the situation from a position of distant doubt and objectification.[9] A hermeneutical approach designed to discover the real Jesus of the Gospels will somewhere have to discover him as "thou" in a conversion that follows the path to "we."

Such responsiveness leads to accurate interpretation. Exploring what "we" means in the context of love and creative fidelity, Marcel turns to a phenomenological analysis of the

[7]Ibid., 33–34.
[8]Ibid., 36.
[9]Ibid., 37.

words "belonging and disposability."[10] These terms he describes as personal act in which we evoke a situation of welcoming another person as a participant in our work and in the undertaking to which we have given ourselves. It is the opposite of claiming selfishly that we belong exclusively to ourselves. This in the end is a self-defeating assertion because the unrelated "I" negates the possibility of any specifiable context. Belonging to others and being at their disposal, however, is characteristic of Jesus' own self-understanding as he lives out the role of servant on behalf of others.[11] Similarly, Jesus' call is that his disciples be servants of others. He also invokes in them a deep sense of admiration, which tears them away from their inner inertia and selfishness. Admiration for Jesus promises an irruption of generosity in those who are not closed, like Jesus' adversaries, to something wonderfully new.[12]

"More precisely," Marcel writes, ". . . I shall say that admiration is related to the fact that something is revealed. Indeed, the ideas of admiration and revelation are correlative."[13] The refusal to admire and the inability to admire, he observes, are characteristic of our age, with its "tendency to view with suspicion any acknowledged mark of superiority." Underlying this suspicion is a burning preoccupation with the self: "But what about me, what becomes of me in that case?"[14] The refusal to admire need not always be based on jealousy or resentment, however; admiration and enthusiasm may be suspect by the critical intellect on the ground that they abolish self-control. But critical intelligence can only help one to understand and to discriminate the facts one subsequently appraises: it cannot *appreciate* or help one decide whether a work or a person is worthy of admiration. The ability to admire is a deeper spiritual response to another, the "affirmation of a superiority that is not

---

[10]Ibid., 38–57; See especially 40.

[11]See Royce Gordon Gruenler, *The Trinity in the Gospel of John*, for an exposition of the theme of disposability in the Gospel of John.

[12]See Marcel's remarks on admiration, *Creative Fidelity*, 47–48.

[13]Ibid., 48.

[14]Ibid.

relative but absolute; absolute, I repeat; the word *incomparable* has a clearly distinct meaning in this context."[15]

In applying this observation to gospel interpretation, one might say that a truer appraisal of Jesus would be guided by an attitude of admiration; here is incomparable superiority. One cannot walk heavily over such art and expect to understand it. It is required of the appreciative interpreter that one be responsive, not scrutinizing the Gospels with the goal of having or possessing them by means of an impersonal critical key, as though one were a file clerk filing facts in drawers and having them at command. Such a model proves inadequate and false, for neither Jesus nor the Gospels nor any work of art yields its secrets to the record-file approach. As long as one refuses to be open and responsive to the personal claims of Jesus, one is, to use Marcel's expression, "captive of the category of causality," with its illusory claim to objective neutrality and its penchant for explaining everything behaviorally and secularly:

> However it may also turn out that submerging oneself suddenly in the life of another person and being forced to see things through his eyes, is the only way of eliminating the self-obsession from which one has sought to free oneself. Alone, one cannot succeed in this, but the presence of the other person accomplishes this miracle, provided one gives one's consent to it and does not treat it as a simple intrusion—but as a reality. Nothing is more free in the true sense of this term, than this acceptance and consent; and there is nothing which is less compatible with the sort of antecedent deliberation which an obsolescent psychology holds as the necessary condition of the free act. The truth is that as long as one is captive to the category of causality, so difficult to apply to the spiritual life, one will not be able to distinguish between coercion and appeal, or between the distinctive modalities of response each of these evokes from us. In my opinion, the word "response" should be reserved for the holy inner reaction evoked by an appeal.[16]

Jesus invites our acceptance and consent to his personal claims and further invites us to see reality through his eyes, as

---

[15]Ibid. His emphasis.
[16]Ibid., 51.

one who is speaking and acting with the authority of God. Only by a person's sympathetic and imaginative openness to Jesus' claims can gospel criticism be freed from mechanical theologies that limit him to natural causality. Such theories claim objectivity but paralyze the image of Jesus for the present as well as for the future. An unwillingness to respond to the appeal of Jesus on the personal level of meeting results in an inner inertia and indisposability. One's interest should not be allowed to dote on theories, like something clutched in a dead hand. This is what religious belief had become for Jesus' opponents; and this is what speculations about gospel origins and the self-understanding of Jesus become in the hands of critics when Jesus is not allowed to make his appeal because he is already assumed to be inaccessible as a self-conscious and self-understanding person. Such doctrines lead to a radical indisposability to Jesus as incarnate "thou." Jesus as distant "he" or "him" is the controllable and malleable figure who is reducible to naturalistic causes without remainder.

Creative disposability, on the other hand, characterizes the work Jesus brings to fruition as he embodies his vocation in redemptive service to others. That is why the Gospels cannot be seen as isolatable stories apart from the self-conscious vision of Jesus as person. Indeed, his works and words are indwelled by his personal "I" and disclose his deepest intentionality. Hence one cannot discover the real Jesus of the Gospels merely by inserting him into a web of objective relations that contain him as a distant "him." Jesus becomes manageable and exhaustible, without remainder, insofar as we construe his life as something wholly quantifiable. The paradox of Jesus' disposability toward the interpreter and the interpreter's disposability toward him is accordingly a major problem in gospel interpretation.[17] This problem does not find its solution in neutral objectivism, which denatures the text and detaches the interpreter as mere specta-

[17]Marcel refers to this general hermeneutical problem as the "metaproblematic of mystery, which I continue to regard as fundamental and which, if improperly construed, will give rise to the most harmful interpretation. There is always a danger of interpreting a mystery as a shallow agnosticism of the end of the nineteenth century." Ibid., 56.

tor. Rather, the solution is in personal openness to Jesus' offer of forgiveness of sins and acceptance of his invitation to participate in open table-fellowship, which characterizes the faithful exegete of God's Word. It is only in the act of disposability as a believer that the interpreter actually experiences a real fusion of his horizon with the horizon of Jesus, who inaugurates in his own person the saving reign of God. That is, genuine interpretation of the deeper meaning of Jesus and the Gospels requires that the exegete be a believer. Otherwise one is only making gestures.

Marcel describes the phenomenon of action contrasted with mere gesturing. Acts are indicative of one's self-revealing; gestures are not. Once again we gain valuable insight into Jesus' "I" as it is disclosed in action and into the "I" of the believer in the act of faith: "An act, I shall maintain, is more an act to the degree that it is impossible to repudiate it without completely denying oneself."[18] Two points stand out in Marcel's phenomenology of personal act. The first is that an act is inconceivable without a personal reference to *I*: "It is I who . . . ." Hence a description of Jesus' acts is tantamount to his saying, "It is I who am doing this and in so doing I disclose who I am." Second, "the act only presents its character of act to the agent or to whoever mentally adopts, through sympathy, the point of the agent."[19] Thus there are two lines of action: one proceeds from the actor, in this case Jesus, whose "I" is demonstrated in his bodily action; the other is a receptive activity, as the gospel interpreter sympathetically and faithfully adopts the point of view of Jesus the agent. In this meeting there is an ever-present danger that the exegete will want to objectify Jesus' act in any given setting as a historical nonact (e.g., by claiming that the church piously created this "happening"), thus removing Jesus' creative "I," which stands behind and within the speech-act.

Marcel warns that our modern tendency to objectify is so strong that we inevitably want to represent an act to ourselves as an effect of some other cause, and to ask who or what caused

[18]Ibid., 109.
[19]Ibid., 108.

it. The biblical critic may want to attribute a number of Jesus' speech-acts to the apologetic concerns of the evangelist in his later churchly setting. This reading of the text does not allow a historical basis to Jesus' acts, hence they do not specify who he really is and what he envisages as his horizon of intention. As a unique and creative person according to the gospel accounts, Jesus specifies concretely who he is when he envisages, appraises, and confronts a situation with courage, exposes himself to determinate action, and assumes responsibility for that action.[20] By his acts and words Jesus makes certain claims and disclosures about himself and reveals his intentional *I*. In gospel criticism today the crisis is precisely regarding which speech-acts will be allowed to identify the historical Jesus. Inevitably, without confidence in Jesus' total claims and the historical reportage of the evangelists, criticism that is motivated by liberal presuppositions will contract out all theologically offensive speech-acts and attribute them to the church.

There is a need in the circles of biblical criticism to allow Jesus to appear as he intentionally claims to be in the complementary gospel accounts. When radical criticism assumes the law of natural causality in the creation of sayings and acts of Jesus by the early church, it reveals its own intentionality of doubt regarding the reliability of the evangelists as faithful witnesses to what Jesus has said and done. Much modern gospel criticism no longer evinces faith in the validity and inspiration of the biblical texts, but advances theories about the natural evolution and historical reliability of those texts. Marcel distinguishes between opinion and faith, defining opinion as detachment and nonparticipation and defining faith as its opposite. "It should be noted at once that we do not have an opinion, strictly speaking, of those beings with whom we are intimately acquainted. . . : The more a state of affairs concerns me, the less I can say in the strict sense of the term that I have an opinion of it."[21]

It would not be off the mark to suggest that evangelicals,

---

[20]See Marcel's description of these personal actions, ibid., 114, 117.
[21]Ibid., 122, 129.

and especially those who have been converted (as I have been) from the presuppositions of liberal theology, feel a certain sense of sadness that there are gospel critics who are dubious that Jesus ever made many of the claims attributed to him in the Gospels. Such depersonalized interpretations entail "that I have an opinion about the universe only to the extent that I disengage myself from it (where I withdraw from the venture without loss)."[22] In critical objectivism, without faith in Jesus as Savior and Lord, one is tied to nonparticipation with the living texts of the Gospels. The believer who exegetes from faith, however, while perhaps open to various theories as to the historical contexts and process of selection by which the evangelists composed their gospels, has that essential quality of openness and faith in the historical story of Jesus that allows Jesus' authentic person to be visualized through the primary authority of eyewitness accounts. The more one is concerned for the message of the Gospels and the primary speaker who is Jesus, the less one has a theoretical opinion about the historicity of the material and the more one passes from the sphere of opinion to the sphere of faith.[23] The sphere of faith or belief is interpreted by Marcel to mean that one opens a credit account to someone. One says, "I freely put myself in your hands; it is as though I freely substituted your freedom for my own; or, paradoxically, it is by that substitution that I realize my freedom." Or, "I welcome you as a participant in my work, in the undertaking to which I have given myself."[24]

This giving or lending or rallying oneself to another is an essentially mysterious act that is personal. The "I" is believing in a "thou," not a thing; for "one can only trust a 'thou.' "[25] Thing-language is impersonal and distant and is essentially problem-oriented. But as Marcel observes, "As long as we think in terms of a problem we will see nothing, understand

---

[22]Ibid., 129.

[23]Ibid., 130.

[24]Ibid., 40; cf. 134.

[25]Ibid., 135. Note the similarity of this hermeneutical insight to the epistemology of Michael Polanyi, *Personal Knowledge*. (Chicago: Univ. of Chicago, 1974). See below, chap. 7.

nothing."[26] The drama and mystery of the gospel story, however, focus on Jesus as the personal embodiment of God's saving reign, and accordingly in reading and interpreting the story one is compelled to make certain commitments to him as he meets us in the drama. This paradox of participation is a striking phenomenon in the Gospels, for the one who meets us on the gospel pages is the very one who places himself at our disposal, has as it were faith in us, gives and rallies and extends his credit to us, and thus is eminently qualified to call us to place ourselves at his disposal and to give and rally and extend our credit to him.

As long as we stand distantly aloof from the text, however, and think of it in terms of a problem, we will see nothing, understand nothing. In the openness of faith, however, the interpreter is confronted by the incarnate Jesus and discovers God's unconditional love for the creature, a gift that will not be revoked.[27] Jesus becomes vulnerable love by placing himself at my disposal. My appropriate response, therefore, is obedience to the text in the sense of obedience to the one who becomes incarnate through the text. The deep meaning of the gospel comes alive again when I reciprocally place myself at Jesus' disposal in loving belief.

One of Marcel's most imaginative and appropriable insights for exegesis is his description of the phenomenon of "creative fidelity," the title of his book of essays. This is bound up with the act of faith and is inseparable from sound New Testament hermeneutics. It is in the plenitude of mystery, Marcel writes, that creative fidelity plays its role, where the loved one is present as "thou": "Fidelity truly exists only where it defies absence, when it triumphs over absence, and in particular, over that absence which we hold to be—mistakenly no doubt—absolute, and which we call death."[28] The real hermeneutical struggle in gospel interpretation is to keep the personally indwelled text from falling continually into the state

[26]Marcel, *Creative Fidelity*, 135.
[27]Ibid., 136.
[28]Ibid., 152.

of a problem and third-person abstraction, where the central person of the text, Jesus, is taken to be essentially absent. This in effect causes the story to die for the reader; the figure of Jesus recedes to a "he" or "it" and becomes the object of critical manipulation, rather than being allowed to address the interpreter in personal terms of "I am" and "thou." In that critical mood, the person of Jesus who invests his words and acts with the authority of "I am" and is personally present in those words and acts, is simply contracted out as one who addresses the interpreter with creative fidelity and offers redemption or judgment and a compelling choice to believe or not to believe.

Creative fidelity is characterized first, says Marcel, by a constancy that must be affirmed ceaselessly by the will in opposition to whatever would threaten it.[29] Second, creative fidelity reveals a mysterious kind of presence that dissipates any feeling of staleness that might arise from constancy. Presence is the sense that another is with me as a friend who is faithful.[30] Third, fidelity offers an essential element of spontaneity, which is truly an imaginative love not born of sheer duty or constancy.[31] This spontaneity always operates on the fundamental commitment to the other, for "the fact is that when I commit myself, I grant in principle that the commitment will not again be put in question."[32] This bars a certain number of possibilities (e.g., "when in doubt, discard") that are demoted to the rank of temptation. Fourth, creative fidelity presupposes both a compelling commitment and an expectation that finds its source in God. It is an essential consecration: "It cannot be a matter of counting on oneself, or on one's own resources, to cope with this unbounded commitment; but in the act in which I commit myself, I at the same time extend an infinite credit to Him to whom I did so. Hope means nothing more than this."[33]

Creative fidelity as a hermeneutical attitude entails a redirection of critical methodology, since critical tools can be

[29]Ibid., 153.
[30]Ibid., 153–54.
[31]Ibid., 155ff.
[32]Ibid., 162.
[33]Ibid., 167.

used constructively as well as destructively. This means that "I believe" should be paramount in the constructive use of biblical criticism if one is a believing Christian and is in the service of the church. In the case of atheistic criticism, where critical tools serve a methodology of doubt with respect to Scripture's authoritative claims, the "I believe" is committed to a philosophy radically different from classical Christianity, and constitutes another gospel that compels criticism in a direction inimical to evangelical faith. The problem of naturalistic New Testament criticism is that it has followed the path of doubt to the point where Christian faith, from which the gospel story arose in the first place, has itself appeared as a problem. The underlying problem, however, is that skeptical criticism does not clearly know what it believes, but is tacitly if not focally antagonistic to the faith of the evangelists. Jesus becomes problematic for modern naturalism, which has voided the supranormal in history and personal commitment to Jesus Christ as Lord and has contracted them out of gospel exegesis. Yet by his speech-acts Jesus claims to be standing in the place of God. Unbelieving criticism, however, refers such claims to the belief of the early church. This is symptomatic of the negative faith of radical doubt that opposes the incarnate vision and authority of Jesus, and the integrity of his witnesses. But by viewing the evangelists' witness to Jesus as a problem, "we tend to intellectualize it, i.e., to falsify it; hence to see in belief an imperfect and even impure mode of knowing. . . ."[34]

The problem lies rather in the modern attitude of unbelief and incredulity, which causes the doubting critical intelligence to analyze all personal language with secular inquiry. According to the Scriptures, this doubt arises from a certain pride in one's reason, and such pride is sinful because it questions the historical integrity of the gospel story.[35] For the believer, the story itself and supremely the One who tells it and embodies it as incarnate "thou" are like a light that requires the interpreter or critic to be receptive, transparent, and reflecting. Unbeliev-

[34]Ibid., 170.
[35]Ibid.

ing criticism is opaque; the believing interpreter is translucent. Marcel observes that "insofar as I am not transparent, I do not believe," for belief is expressed in respect of translucent love and charity.[36] Modern skeptical gospel criticism therefore betrays overconfidence in autonomous reason and its ability to sort out answers to problems in abstraction, without reference to God's authoritative revelation. The method of positivism questions every claim to truth and puts it to the test by some "objective" criterion that is assumed to be neutral and free of personal prejudice or commitment. Marcel trenchantly criticizes this malaise of Western Enlightenment intellectualism: "Rationalism has introduced an abstract element into human relations which depersonalizes beings. . . ."[37]

Marcel proposes a hermeneutical methodology that is reflectively empirical and encompasses the wider scope of historical phenomena, including divine revelation. Interpersonal experience and convivial participation in the life of others are central, Marcel argues, to discovering the plenitude of a text and experiencing renewal through it. Applied to Jesus and the Gospels, Marcellian phenomenology would focus on a descriptive exegesis of Jesus' project to restore the brokenness of persons in a fallen world. Phenomenological exegesis would describe the spoken and acted language that he indwells and that embodies him as he inaugurates the kingdom of God, bringing redemption, recuperation, and participation. It would further describe his characteristic claim to offer divine forgiveness in terms of open table-fellowship and redemptive suffering. Since Jesus' *I* is embodied in his speech-acts, a faithful and accepting reading of those words and acts allows the exegete to be confronted by the incarnate Jesus as he is speaking and acting in the original accounts of the evangelists.

Since Jesus appears in the Gospels as incarnate being, his "I" reveals his awareness of a special messiahship. Jesus' self-understanding is "manifestory" and has civil status.[38] Through

---

[36]Ibid., 172.

[37]Ibid., 8–9.

[38]I am indebted to Robert Rosenthal's summary introduction in ibid., ix–xxvi, especially xvi-xvii on this point.

the Gospels, which bear witness to his spoken and acted language, we glimpse his self-understanding, his vision, horizon, "existential orbit"—in short, his personal pronoun *I*. Jesus' *I* is made known by his openness, disposability, and permeability on behalf of those he came to save. The exegete who approaches Jesus' spiritual availability with love, fidelity, and interpersonal communion will be confronted by Jesus' very intentionality through the text. Thus faithfulness, sympathy, feeling with Jesus, and placing oneself at his disposal makes one copresent and "at home" with him.

Jesus' language extends a sensation of receptivity and hospitality to the interpreter who comes as a believer and invites a resonant response of love and trust. Accurate exegesis of Jesus and his language is not attainable, therefore, from the distant detachment of the mere spectator. The spectator model, which arises from radical criticism's desire to be "scientific," is accompanied by emotions of distrust ("when in doubt, discard"), disbelief, impermeability, and indisposability. That is not to say that scientific objectivity of the right kind does not have its role to play in the analysis of Jesus' embodied language. Indeed, Jesus can become truly objective only when the intellect has first acknowledged him as Savior and Lord. The scientific habit, Marcel knows, can be abused and can lead to depersonalizing and dehumanizing. Objectivism in gospel criticism has often followed the problematic approach (the Gospels are a "problem," Jesus is a "problem") and in so doing has eliminated mystery, excluded revelation as a source for truth, rejected the supranormal, and excluded personal belief and commitment. Only by allowing these components their proper role in the exegesis of Jesus' *I*-embodied language can the interpreter make proper response to Jesus' claims and to his appeal and offer accurate and objective exegesis.

A study of Marcel's hermeneutics of fidelity and disposability implies that good gospel interpretation requires the interpreter to be open and responsive to the claims of Jesus, as disclosed in his words and acts. But the biblical interpreter must undergo repentance in the sphere of the intellect if he or she is to use the tools of analysis constructively. Anything less leads ultimately to a serious misunderstanding of Jesus the Speaker who embodies his revelatory and redeeming *I* in the folds of his spoken and acted story.[39]

[39]See ibid., xxvi, 173.

Part 2

HERMENEUTICS FROM THE PERSPECTIVE OF ANGLO-AMERICAN REALISM

5
BRITISH SCHOOLS OF REALISM

It has been noted that Continental idealism made its mark upon a segment of British intellectualism in the last third of the nineteenth century and substantially influenced American thought as well. The names of T. H. Green, F. H. Bradley, Bernard Bosanquet, and C. A. Campbell in Britain and Josiah Royce in America are representative of prominent philosophical figures who adapted German idealism to the traditions of the English-speaking world. Yet idealism, however widespread its influence continues to be in hermeneutical circles among Anglo-American as well as Continental biblical scholars, does not represent the most distinctive contribution of English and American philosophical thought to hermeneutical method. This is to be found rather in its traditional emphasis on practical realism and empirical methodology.

For that reason part 2 will not replicate strains of German idealism transplanted into English soil but will concentrate on specific schools of Anglo-American empiricism and realism that offer creative possibilities for biblical hermeneutics. While several of the figures to be considered, like Wittgenstein and Polanyi, were not native to the English-speaking idiom, the particular strain of their later writings is valuable in view of their adaptation of the practical realism that could have sprung up only on British soil in reaction to the dominant idealism on the Continent.

Common-sense realism appeared early in Britain in the writings of the Scottish philosophers Francis Hutcheson (1694–1746), and Thomas Reid (1710–1796), who wrote in criticism of the empirical idealism of Berkeley and the skepticism of Hume. While common sense philosophy contains its own set of problems (e.g., its naïveté concerning the role of presuppositions and the relativity of perspectives), it has always had a strong though often tacit presence in British thought. New schools of realism emerge in the twentieth century, but begin badly with a revolt against not only idealism but religion as well. It is important, however, to note the contributions as well as the weaknesses of the new nontheistic realism that emerged in the early part of the twentieth century, before moving to more mature expressions of empirical realism which appeared a generation or two later. It must be borne in mind that while realism is not inherently inimical to religion (certainly not to biblical revelation, as we shall see), its modern expressions are often allied with naturalism and pragmatism and tend to give more weight to materialism than to mind and value, as in idealism. For that reason the early realisms of the twentieth century do not carry the day and must undergo the more searching analysis and creative synthesis of hermeneutical points of view that emerge by the middle of the century.

Non-Theistic Realism: G. E. Moore, Bertrand Russell. It was G. E. Moore (1873–1958) who revived common-sense realism in reaction to the idealism that had pervaded Britain by the turn of the century. The central thrust of his work was the thesis that the mind does not constitute reality but discovers it, and that objects are there just as truly when they are not observed as when they are. The revival of this commonsensible notion which lay people would not normally think to question, created a considerable stir in intellectual circles. Among orthodox Christians, however, a realism informed by Scripture continued to afford a strong philosophical position because it attests the reality of God apart from the observing mind and affirms the objective reality of the creation God has brought into being and sustains by the word of his power.

Moore rejected both theology and metaphysics and felt

constrained to avoid speculations on larger issues. He was not able to develop any comprehensive view of reality, but limited himself mainly to pursuing linguistic problems of logic. His major venture into ethics (*Principia Ethica*)[1] fails to provide a basis for "good" as a simple fact since he denies any absolute, including the biblical definition of good. Yet he is obliged to borrow from the Judaeo-Christian ethical tradition to rescue his humanism from slipping into subjective idealism. Nonetheless, his intuition of an objective reality beyond the knowing mind performed the helpful task of steering British philosophical thought back to its common-sense origins. It would require someone with a wider ranging epistemology, however, to sustain the shift to realism—someone committed to a biblical view of the world as created and sustained by God, who is the source of all real knowledge of the self and of objects.

Bertrand Russell (1872–1964) continued the drift of the new realism into smaller objective units of analysis with his philosophy of logical atomism. He interpreted reality as a universe composed of many independent entities with mathematical and logical relationships. These relationships, he held, must be understood mainly through science and logic.[2] Unlike Moore, however, Russell was also interested in the larger canvas and painted with broad brush strokes, working from the minute world of atoms logically arranged (oddly, by *chance*), to large pronouncements on the absence of God in a universe without ultimate purpose or meaning.[3]

Russell illustrates a fundamental inconsistency in contemporary philosophical hermeneutics. The origin and destiny of the universe is due on the one hand to the "accidental collocations of atoms" and is therefore ultimately morally evil,

---

[1]G. E. Moore, *Principia Ethica* (Cambridge: University Press, 1903). See also idem, *Some Main Problems of Philosophy* (New York: Macmillan, 1953); idem, *Philosophical Studies* (New York: Littlefield, Adams, 1959).

[2]Bertrand Russell, *Our Knowledge of the External World* (New York: New American Library, 1960); idem, with Alfred North Whitehead, *Principia Mathematica*, 3 vols. (Cambridge: University Press, 1925).

[3]Bertrand Russell, *Mysticism and Logic* (London: Allen & Unwin, 1917); idem, *Why I Am Not a Christian and Other Essays* (London: Allen & Unwin, 1957).

because it destroys life. On the other hand it is a rational and logical universe that is capable of scientific verification by the human mind. This is an irrational philosophical position, not untypical of modern humanism. According to Russell, scientific truthfulness and human ideals alone are worthy of respect; yet he posits no metaphysical or biblical basis on which to establish such universal statements about the nature of reality. In light of Paul's realistic description of the state of fallen creation in Romans 1:19–23, the "realism" of Russell would fall under the category of the great exchange, by which the self-revealed glory of God through common grace in creation is exchanged for the glory of the human mind. In light of the logical contradictions in his view of the universe, Russell is in practice closer to idealism than to realism, since he imagines that an ultimately irrational and meaningless universe is capable of responding to the rational categories of logical atomism and human idealism. His philosophy in the end is an effort to create hope out of hopelessness, a truth he virtually recognizes when he coins the phrase "unyielding despair" to describe the human quest for meaning and significance.[4] In this respect he has hardly advanced over the naturalism and skepticism of his empiricist predecessor, Hume.

Nevertheless, Russell has hold of something that is not only logical but of considerable importance in the formation of scientific method, namely, the symmetry and regularity of the created world, which discloses itself in the day-to-day realities of scientific analysis, making possible the harnessing of enormous power in the twentieth century. Idealism cannot account for the remarkable scientific conformity of the mind to objective reality nor the response of nature to the categories of the mind. The intuition of an objective reality that reveals itself to the human mind finds a more adequate philosophical justification in Polanyi's theistically informed hermeneutics (see chapter 7). It is ironic that in his last years Russell seemed close

[4]Russell, *Mysticism and Logic*, 44–45. "Confident despair" is an alternative phrase.

to repenting of his earlier ideological atheism and materialism, though with what specific consequences we cannot be certain.

Metaphysical Realism. Several spokesmen of the new realism recognized the vulnerability of realism to the criticisms of idealism if larger spiritual issues were not somehow accommodated. Philosophical analysis alone would not suffice. Mild ventures into the fringe area of psychic research were suggested by C. D. Broad and H. H. Price as possible evidence for human survival after death.[5] These were odd whistlings in the dark, however, and were accompanied by rejection of the empirical claim of Scripture that the resurrection of Jesus Christ ensures the resurrection of believers at the end of the age. Both Broad and Price dismissed belief in a personal God and, like Moore and Russell, adopted realism's variation of Kantian dualism. They fashioned the world according to the ideals of materialist scientism on the factual side, while exercising subjective imagination of a psychical nature at the value pole. These nontheistic realists were realists in theory only; in practice they were closet idealists who superimposed their categories of meaning upon a reality that could be known only on the grounds of their own epistemology. Without belief in God and his revelation in nature and Scripture there could be no adequate basis for the knowability of the facts in themselves and no antidote to Kant's skepticism concerning the noumenal facts in themselves. Broad and Price accordingly illustrate the recurrent truth that wherever God does not play a dominant role in a philosophical system, its epistemology will revert to a form of Kantian dualism and finally to skepticism. In spite of early twentieth-century realism's appeals to common sense, it could not sustain itself in the fires of radical criticism without God, as Broad and Price unwittingly attest.

More systematic realists, however, began to move in the direction of metaphysical realism and the reintroduction of deity in some form to the objective process of the empirical

---

[5]C. D. Broad, *Religion, Philosophy and Scientific Research* (London, 1953); idem, *Lectures on Psychical Research* (London, 1963); H. H. Price, "Psychical Research and Human Personality," *Hibbert Journal* 47 (1948–49): 105–13.

world, reforming the claims of absolute idealism on the grounds of realism. Process realism emphasized the role of the natural sciences, the ultimacy of time and space, and the relative importance of mind, unlike idealist metaphysics which highlighted absolute mind as constitutive of a reality outside time and space. Process and becoming now pressed forward to the leading edge of a new speculative philosophical realism. Typical of the new group of speculative realists was C. Lloyd Morgan (1852–1936), a zoologist and philosopher who conceived of the real world as emergent evolutionary novelty that is not reducible to predictable patterns of physics, chemistry, and mechanism. The world emerges in three great stages from the physico-chemical, to the vital, to the mental, guided by the orderly process of God.[6] Morgan's realism was uneasily dualistic, however. It was fashioned essentially out of naturalism and wedded to a world of spirit and deity beyond the emergent evolutionary process that guided it along and manifested itself within the process.

A contemporary of Morgan in the school of metaphysical realism, Samuel Alexander (1859–1938), attempted to avoid Morgan's dualism by positing emergent evolution as the absolute from which everything, including deity, emerges. This emergence evolves in four stages out of primal space-time stuff: first matter, then life, then mind, and finally deity emerge successively.[7] Objective qualities reside in the entities themselves, not in states of mind, as the space-time process moves inexorably forward toward its goal of deification. God is the end of evolution, not its beginning, and is totally within nature, not outside it, as in Morgan's metaphysical system. Everything has its physical and mental aspects, including God. On the physical side, God's body is comprised pantheistically of the whole network of finite space-time, while on the mental side, deity evolves to transcendence.

The biblical interpreter will find little here that correlates

---

[6]C. Lloyd Morgan, *Emergent Evolution* (London, 1923); idem, *Life, Mind, and Spirit* (London, 1926).

[7]Samuel Alexander, *Space, Time, and Deity*, 2 vols. (London, 1920).

with either the self-revelation of God in Scripture as eternally sovereign and transcendent, or his relation to nature as creator and sustainer. In light of biblical hermeneutics, Alexander's notion of a space-time deity seems to be more a speculative accommodation to modern evolutionary naturalism than a faithful reading of the nature of reality itself. Compared to Morgan's scheme of evolutionary emergence, Alexander's emergent evolution suffers from want of a guiding mind or principle to ensure that primal space-time will finally produce God.

The most imaginative and influential of the metaphysical realists was Alfred North Whitehead (1861–1947), whose *Process and Reality* remains one of the great speculative studies of the twentieth century.[8] Along with his other important works, it is one of the most serious challenges to historic Christianity and biblical hermeneutics in modern times. I have dealt at length with the process theism of Whitehead and his disciple Charles Hartshorne (along with other contemporary process philosophers) in *The Inexhaustible God: Biblical Faith and the Challenge of Process Theism.*[9] From Bertrand Russell, with whom he collaborated on *The Principles of Mathematics (Principia Mathematica*, 1903), Whitehead adopted the doctrine of logical atomism, which holds that the most basic units of reality are atomic. From this doctrine he developed a comprehensive view of the universe based on atomic occasions that emerge, peak, perish, and furnish data for the next processive wave of creativity. Every individual event on every level of intensity is a unique emergent and actual entity that freely adds its own novelty to the extensive continuum of evolutionary advance. This creative advance on a cosmic scale is lured on (but not sovereignly guided) by the ideals of God for maximum feeling and beauty. The universe is dynamically in process. In general outline, Whitehead's process theism resembles the Continental empirical realism of the Austrian philosopher Franz Brentano

[8]Alfred North Whitehead, *Process and Reality: An Essay in Cosmology* (New York: Harper & Row, 1957).

[9]Royce Gordon Gruenler, *The Inexhaustible God: Biblical Faith and the Challenge of Process Theism* (Grand Rapids: Baker, 1983).

(1838–1917),[10] who held not only to the major tenet of realism that every mental act has an intentional character because it refers beyond itself to real objects, but also to a belief similar to Whitehead's that God himself advances within the temporal process.

In Whitehead's system every entity from God downward has a physical pole and a mental pole and is therefore bipolar. God has his mental pole, or primordial unconscious nature, which offers conceptual lures for actualization by the lesser entities of the universe. When these entities so choose (not necessarily consciously) to make the divine ideals actual, God experiences concrete satisfaction and advancement in his physical or consequent nature. Accordingly, God is both absolute and relative, transcendent and immanent, infinite and finite, depending on which pole of his bipolarity one focuses attention. These divine attributes are not interpreted by Whitehead in traditional biblical terms, however. Whitehead's primordial deity, while eternal, is unconscious and deficient of actual content and serves mainly to provide a range of possibilities by way of eternal objects that function as lures to creativity. The consequent God, on the other hand, has actual content and is conscious, but is incomplete because he is forever surpassing himself as he advances in the world process. The principle of creativity, however, is the actual container of the two-natured God and of the entire processing universe. Creativity accounts for the everlasting novelty that, above all else, Whitehead esteems as absolutely necessary to preserve the freedom of atomic entities (emergent occasions) that contribute to the advance of the universe. The actual, conscious God is therefore finite because he is limited to the process of time and space and must depend on some universe or other everlastingly. The universe provides the content of God's actual and conscious experience, which is socially interwoven like a nexus or web with all emergent occasions.

There are serious problems in Whitehead's metaphysical

[10]Portions of Brentano's *Psychologie* are translated in R. M. Chisholm, ed., *Realism and the Background of Phenomenology* (Glencoe, Ill., 1960).

realism, which I have critiqued in *The Inexhaustible God.* Whitehead adamantly dismisses historic Christianity and the biblical claim that God is sovereign over creation as its creator and sustainer. His major hermeneutical concern is to preserve the freedom of the individual and his right to make novel and unanticipated choices, thus explaining his need of a finite deity who must interact with the contributions of atomic entities. At the same time, Whitehead subscribes to evolutionary theory and must ensure that atomic choices throughout the universe do not end in chaos; hence his need of the primordial God who unconsciously lures the universe onward and upward forever in creative advance. Further problems in process theism will be discussed when American versions of the process school are considered.

These criticisms notwithstanding, there is one major focus in process thought that draws from the biblical tradition and illuminates a fundamental fact that is of considerable significance for biblical hermeneutics and exegesis. This is process philosophy's insistence on the social nature of reality. Unfortunately, process theism mistakenly rejects the social nature of the triune God prior to and apart from creation because its liberal presuppositions require that the divine sociality be linked of necessity with the processing universe, i.e., God needs a universe for the content of his social experience. This view requires a modal or symbolic trinitarianism, since it rules out the eternal ontological Trinity. As I have tried to demonstrate in a thematic exegesis of the Gospel of John,[11] the dialogues of Jesus evidence a dynamic and inexhaustible social relationship between Father, Son, and Holy Spirit as one God in divine Community that is prior to and independent of creation. This view is sustained throughout the New Testament, and finds confirmation in the Old Testament.[12]

---

[11]Royce Gordon Gruenler, *The Trinity in the Gospel of John* (Grand Rapids: Baker, 1986).

[12]A second study, *The Trinity in the New Testament*, is in preparation with exegetical documentation of relevant texts. A projected third volume will draw on the social themes that call on God's people to image the redemptive levels of community in human relationships and in the ecological world of nature.

If we may conclude from God's disclosure of himself in Scripture that he is primordially conscious and social and therefore fully actual as one God in the dynamic and inexhaustible interaction of the Persons of Father, Son, and Holy Spirit, then realism is sustained at the highest archetypal level, as well as derivatively at the secondary level of creation. The dynamic one-in-manyness of creation may then be viewed as the gracious outpouring of God's sociality, which bears the creative signature of the dynamic One-in-Many God.

There is another principal difference between a biblical view of sociality and process and Whitehead's speculative metaphysical realism, which dismisses all but the barest accounts of Scripture.[13] A genuinely biblical realism takes seriously the rebellion of humanity against God, God's judgment of the world as a result of sin, the love of God for his world in the gift of Jesus Christ his Son, the vicarious atonement of sinners through the death and resurrection of his Son and faith in that righteous and justifying work, and the hopeful prospect of the eschatological process that leads to resolution with the return of Christ at the end of the age. Whitehead has none of these redemptive social characteristics in his system. According to his naturalistic reading of the evolutionary process, the world goes on forever without final resolution (a modern version of Zoroastrianism). Humanity redeems itself by responding to the divine lures to beauty, but only temporarily, for death ends all creative actuality for every atomic occasion. Everything perishes upon peaking and is lost forever, except perhaps in the memory of God.

That is certainly not a biblical view. Process thought begins in optimism and ends in pessimism, the opposite of Christian belief. Process theism's Pelagian agenda reduces the sovereign God of Scripture to a limited deity who has to work with independent entities in a world process not ultimately under his control. The school nevertheless encourages the

---

[13]Whitehead holds to a prevailing liberal view of Jesus the Galilean in *Religion in the Making* (Cambridge: University Press, 1926) but rejects the sovereignty of God, the infallibility of Scripture, and other fundamental doctrines of classical Christianity.

exegete to be aware of the social themes of relationship and covenant in Scripture, and especially to appreciate the social nature of God. Scripture's distinctive contribution to social theology is to point to the fact that the dynamic process of sociality in nature stems ultimately from the social God who is One-in-Three and Three-in-One.[14]

Reality is therefore rooted in the social. Sociality is real and ultimate. That is Whitehead's contribution to biblical hermeneutics. The fundamentally social theme of biblical theology needs to be explored and articulated—not so much by way of speculative metaphysics, however, as by careful and responsible exegesis of God's self-revelation in Scripture.

Logical Empiricism: British Analytical Realism. There seems to be a considerable gap between the large systems of the metaphysical realists and the small linguistic foci of the language analysts. Yet as we shall see, the analysts in the school of realism, in spite of their concentration on linguistic minutiae and their sometimes overbearing pronouncements on the irrelevance of religious language, do number in their society certain figures who have made contributions that bear significantly on biblical hermeneutics and exegesis. Most notable are the later Wittgenstein, Peter Strawson, John Searle, and I. T. Ramsey, who have made important statements on persons as agents with public status and the viability of logically odd religious assertions. These important clues to hermeneutical method will be discussed presently.

First it is necessary to say a few words in general about the branch of British realism called logical empiricism, a movement that dominated the field of British philosophy from the 1930s through the 1950s, in reaction both to idealism and metaphysical realism. The large questions were to be left to the empirical and more scientific disciplines, while the focus of philosophy was to be directed to the clarification of meaning through logical analysis of language. Stemming from an earlier logical

[14]Perhaps the book most deserving of the interpreter's attention, and one of the easiest for the beginner to read, is Alfred North Whitehead's *Modes of Thought* (Cambridge: University Press, 1938), a study that lays out the social interconnections of the levels of nature with considerable insight.

positivism that would have nothing to do with "emotive" and therefore empirically unverifiable and meaningless religious statements (since scientific language alone was considered normative),[15] the concerns of logical empiricism have been directed more to the quest for clarification than for truth: "What do you mean by that?" was, and continues to be, a central question of the school.

Ludwig Wittgenstein (1889–1951). The earlier work of this transplanted Austrian engineer was written in the spirit of logical positivism and resembles the thought of Rudolf Carnap of the Vienna Circle. This Circle held that since the scientific method is all-embracing, philosophy serves only as a logical handmaid to clarify scientific concepts and analyze language; it gives no knowledge of the world. In the brash and earlier stage of the *Tractatus*.[16] Wittgenstein went one step further than Carnap (who believed that philosophy could create a scientific metalanguage) and dispensed with philosophy altogether. He argued that the only informative and meaningful propositions are those of the natural sciences that picture the atomic facts of reality in concepts that serve a truth-function. All other propositions are either tautologies (so logic and mathematics) or nonsense (religion, metaphysics). Hence, when philosophy has done its work and said what it has to say by way of clarifying scientific propositions, it should be silent and kick away its own ladder.

At this stage of his thought Wittgenstein was a positivist. Yet he was also committed to a kind of neo-Kantian dualism. While philosophy functioned only at the fact pole to clarify scientific statements, at the pole of subjective feeling an inexpressible mysticism intruded itself into his aphoristic language, much like the nonpropositional mysticism of Otto's phenomenology of religion and the radical Kantian fact/value dualism of Bultmann. While Wittgenstein asserted in the *Tractatus* that God does not reveal himself *in* the world (thus he

---

[15]Representative of the school was A. J. Ayer, *Language, Truth and Logic*, 1936; 2nd rev. ed. (New York: Dover, 1946).

[16]See Ludwig Wittgenstein, *Tractatus Logico-Philosophicus* (1922; reprint, New York: Humanities, 1961).

rejects the incarnational theology of Scripture), there is nevertheless the hint of a wider religious world in his later period when he was closer to realism than to Kantian idealism and would come to realize that religious language is a this-worldly phenomenon bound up with the forms of human life in the public arena of discourse.

After a hiatus of some years from the world of philosophy, Wittgenstein reopened his quest for philosophical meaning in the early 1930s, this time with greater descriptive sensitivity for the various "language games" and "forms of life" that persons experience in their relationships. In cryptic aphorisms[17] he abandons the narrower positivism of the *Tractatus* and opens up the analysis of discourse to everyday language-games. In *Jesus, Persons, and the Kingdom of God* (1967) and in *New Approaches to Jesus and the Gospels* (1982) I have taken Wittgenstein's descriptive insights concerning the way persons speak and convey meaning and have applied them to the person of Jesus as he functions in the gospel narratives. A canny observer of what he calls the forms of life, Wittgenstein investigates ordinary discourse where persons as subjects preside. He is especially opposed to the modern tendency to treat the knower either as a thing or as a passive recipient or as both—a viewpoint that tends to bracket out the function of the knower himself. As was noted of Heidegger and his successors (see chapter 3), a modern fascination with language has led many philosophers and theologians to apotheosize speech as something independent of persons speaking. Hence the personal dimension of language disappears, and things begin to be separated from their names.

Wittgenstein is concerned about such reductionism and the skepticism with which the modern specialist tends to reduce everything to impersonal abstractions. As we will see Polanyi arguing later, more trenchantly and systematically, Wittgenstein insists that language is grounded in its civil status and in

[17]Gathered posthumously in *Philosophical Investigations* (New York: Macmillan, 1953). For a revealing portrait of Wittgenstein and his complexities, see W. W. Bartley III, *Wittgenstein* (Peru, Ill.: Open Court, 1985).

personal subscription to what is said, since it is as human beings that we participate in the activity of speaking and hearing. This serves as an important reminder of something often overlooked because it is always before our eyes, i.e., that persons indwell their language and reveal their personal intentionality in what they say and do. Without that indwelling, no meaning or understanding is possible. Language is underwritten by persons who speak and act out their intentionality in the public sphere. Language therefore has a personal, social, and historical context and reference:

> When, for example, I use a form of words, I am dwelling in that form of words, and giving my personal signature to them. Insofar as you hear what I am saying and understand what I mean, you may be said to be dwelling in that form of words, too. Without personal, human indwelling, language is no longer living and concrete speech.[18]

In light of Wittgenstein's common-sense approach to embodied speech and action, the speech-acts of Jesus and the importance of his incarnation may be appreciated in a new way. This also informs the biblical disclosure of divine intention as a whole.[19] Biblical authority is neither expressed nor experienced, therefore, outside given language-games. Special revelation assumes the validity of God's common revelation in the fabric of nature and human historical discourse. As Thiselton aptly comments, the language-games of the Bible embrace a whole range of dynamic speech-acts: commanding, promising, asking, judging, blessing, warning, pardoning, acclaiming, and so on. But at another level all these broadly "performative" acts can be effective only because certain states of affairs are true. Thus Jesus can say "Your sins be forgiven you" only because he is the one who can forgive sins. In *this* sense, the authority of the

---

[18]Dallas High, *Language, Persons, and Belief: Studies in Wittgenstein's "Philosophical Investigations" and Religious Uses of Language* (New York: Oxford University Press, 1967), 22.

[19]For an extended discussion of Wittgenstein and an application of his "grammar" to Paul and James, see A. Thiselton, *Two Horizons*, 386–438.

words of Jesus rests on something that lies *behind* the particular speech-act and its interpretation.[20]

The performative language of Scripture functions effectively because the biblical writers assume that a certain state of affairs is true, that is, God is actively and sovereignly disclosing what the nature of the case is. The principal danger of using Wittgenstein's methodology for biblical exegesis is that he himself was not working from belief in the objective data of divine revelation in Scripture. Consequently his analysis of language-games led him and his followers to question any real fixity of meaning (univocity) in the process of the changing forms of life. This opens the door to a simplistic and relativistic equation of meaning with use and the reduction of truth statements to changing human practice. Nevertheless, a selective application of the method to biblical exegesis can be helpful. The themes of learning in the context of community and of evidencing appropriate behavior ("Hear, O Israel . . . ," Deut. 6:1–9; "By their fruit you will recognize them," Matt. 7:16, 20) are fundamental biblical concepts. Persons are identified by the language-games they play in the public domain of human behavior. Jesus himself claims to be the foremost paradigm (John 13:14–7). Kantian dualism and the subjective individualism it fosters in the religious sphere (Bultmann's existentialism, for example) finds a healthy counterpoint in Wittgenstein's insistence on historical tradition and performative public acts. The analysis of speech-acts by Wittgenstein and the subsequent work of P. F. Strawson and J. R. Searle (among others) afford useful aids for biblical hermeneutics and exegesis, as the following section will attempt to demonstrate in further detail.

The Functional Analysis of Speech-Acts: P. F. Strawson and J. R. Searle. One has to be careful not to equate personal intentionality totally with behavioral action, as though public speech-acts exhaust what a person thinks and intends (a reductive behaviorism that creeps into Gilbert Ryle's analysis of

[20]Ibid., 437.

dispositional properties).[21] An analysis of Jesus' speech-acts in the Gospels does not exhaust what went on in his mind any more than reading a person's intentionality from his or her speech-acts totally reduces that person's inner life to public scrutiny. For that reason it is not possible to write an exhaustive life of Jesus or to describe the psychological development of his religious self-consciousness.[22] But Jesus' activity in word and work, as selected by the evangelists from the larger pool of his speech-acts, does reveal his self-understanding as Messiah, Son of Man, and Son of God as it relates to his redemptive task. Jesus makes much of speaking and acting with purity of intention, since a self is known by the fruit of personal activity (Matt. 7:16, 20; John 13:35). Accordingly, an analysis of character traits discerned in Jesus' public behavior is indispensable to understanding his personal intentionality, since individuals are known only insofar as they reveal themselves publicly by means of their traits of character.

The disposition of Jesus as redeeming Messiah is therefore disclosed in his intentional commitment to be disposable to sinners in his life of righteousness, vicarious death, and resurrection from the dead, thereby inaugurating a new age of salvation.[23] Jesus commited himself to empirically observable, testable, and determinable physical actions freely chosen, as he set his face toward accomplishing his redemptive goal.

It is here that we can see the significant difference between the realism of personal intention attested by physical actions and the dualism of Kantian idealism. The latter reduces bodily action in the public sphere to natural causality and personal freedom to the state of subjectivity. This reduction is typical of biblical schools of interpretation that limit the public ministry of the historical Jesus to a bare minimum by radical doubt. The historical speech-acts of Jesus are substantially diminished in number and content and appear mainly at the value pole of the

---

[21]Gilbert Ryle, *The Concept of Mind* (London: Hutchinson, 1949).

[22]E.g., J. R. Michaels, *Servant and Son* (Richmond: John Knox, 1983).

[23]For the development of this theme, see R. G. Gruenler, *New Approaches to Jesus and the Gospels* (Grand Rapids: Baker, 1982); idem, *The Trinity in the Gospel of John*.

interpreter where the existential or political freedom of Jesus affords some paradigm for exercising subjective freedom in making authentic religious choices.[24] The subjectivist language of idealism tends to strip away the historical realism of the Gospels, except as it suits agendas already arrived at from the secular sphere. In fact, however, Jesus' choices as a person are known in his deliberate decision to reveal himself by definite physical performance, of which the evangelists claim to be faithful historical witnesses. Idealist presuppositions in exegesis encourage the elimination of much of the physical actions of Jesus because it is assumed that objective religious truth cannot be disclosed in the sphere of empirical phenomena.

British schools of realism, as we would adapt them to biblical exegesis, reject such idealism with common-sense analysis of how human beings do in fact come to know one another through self-disclosure in the objective and public sphere of speech-acts. Emphasizing the social dimension of reality, realism rejects a mind-body dualism that employs the tools of historical research in gnostic and docetic fashion. P. F. Strawson's analysis of persons[25] makes a bold statement about holistic intentional action that enables one to think of persons as agent organisms and psychophysical units. Strawson purposes to remind us that the most logically primitive idea in our description of individuals is the concept of persons as body-mind unities who are interrelated with other persons. If purely private experiences were all we had to work with in our investigation of states of consciousness, there would be no way of distinguishing one person's experiences from another's. All would be mine and therefore no one's:

> To put it briefly, one can ascribe states of consciousness to oneself only if one can ascribe them to others. One can ascribe them to others only if one can identify other objects of experience. And one cannot identify others if one can identify

---

[24]For a critique of Bultmann, Käsemann, Perrin, and the New Hermeneutic, see Gruenler, *New Approaches*, 34–131.

[25]P. F. Strawson, *Individuals: An Essay in Descriptive Metaphysics* (London: Methuen, 1964). See also J. L. Austin, *How to Do Things with Words*, 2nd ed. (Oxford: Clarendon, 1975).

> them only as subjects of experience, possessors of states of consciousness.[26]

There are two important points in this argument that bear on the interpretation of Jesus' language. The first is that one's self-consciousness as a person is inseparable from one's relationship to others. That is, a person is not a purely isolated ego in the Cartesian sense. The second reflects the Old and New Testament concern that personal intention, word, and act be viewed in holistic fashion and not as separable and independent (as in play-acting or hypocrisy). Strawson reminds us that we come into being as persons only because we are able to relate to others and identify them as incarnate persons with their own unique intentionality, speech, and bodily action. The characteristics that identify another person may be material predicates (Strawson calls them M-predicates), such as "weighs 140 pounds" or "is in the drawing room." Since these descriptions can also be made of material bodies to which states of consciousness are not applied, the more important identifying characteristics of persons are what Strawson calls P-predicates or person predicates, such as "is smiling," "is going for a walk," "is in pain," "is thinking hard," "believes in God," and so on.

In Jesus' case the P-predicates would be "is forgiving someone's sins," "is healing that person," or "is having table-fellowship with those people." His person, hence his intention, is discovered *in* his speech and acts, as is the intention of any other person: "The primary reference of predicates of intention is *not* consciousness, but the bodily, observable action of the person."[27] This is an important hermeneutical insight to bring to bear on gospel exegesis. It corrects the abandoned quests of the historical Jesus, quests that have spent misdirected searches for his inner consciousness and religious development. Rather, the subjectivity of a person is revealed in the objectivity of his behavior:

---

[26]Strawson, *Individuals*, 150.

[27]Robert H. King, "The Concept of the Person," *Journal of Religion 46* (January, 1966), p. 41.

> What we are saying is that a concept of the person which includes objectivity does not thereby desubjectify the person in the sense of denying him subjecthood. Rather it credits the subjecthood of the person in a particularly significant way by indicating its presence in a form intrinsically intelligible to others.[28]

In the simpler language of Jesus, "By their fruit you will recognize them" (Matt. 7:16). Here Jesus expresses his thematic witness to the integral self, to the inner and the outer, to consciousness and body, to subjectivity and objectivity, to intention and the language of activity that is so characteristic of his own words and works. Mind and body are therefore inseparable, as are the subjective/objective poles. Neither can be reduced to the other or separated in compartments as in Cartesian and Kantian dualism. As one can readily see, there are important implications here for the New Testament's insistence on the incarnate reality of Jesus Christ as embodied person in his birth, life, death, and resurrection. The evangelists faithfully narrate the historical speech-acts of a real person. They do not create pious or gnostic fiction in the manner of the dualistic docetists, who held that Jesus only seemed to have a body.

Strawson's analysis of what it means to be a person in historical terms, namely, that a person is an intentional psychophysical organism, could have a salutary effect in challenging the underlying hermeneutics of radical gospel criticism. In light of Strawson's analysis of the speech-acts of embodied persons, radically skeptical interpretations of Jesus appear arbitrarily selective, even gnostic. They assume that the intentional Jesus cannot be known through the portraits of his speech-acts in the Gospels, since these are believed to be highly idealized by the redacting church and are therefore to a large extent unhistorical. Interpreters in this school claim that all that can be known of Jesus is his "idea" of existential self-understanding (idealism). Others with less interest in subjective crises than in social crises involving oppressive political structures view Jesus as a paradigm for political liberation.

At stake are christological questions about Jesus' messianic

[28]Ibid., 42.

self-understanding and his intention to speak and act as he is described in the gospel narratives. The Gospels should not be interpreted by skeptical methodologies that flow from preconceived idealist agendas. Rather, they should be interpreted on the grounds of their own intrinsic testimony as witnesses of Jesus' historical speech-acts. The Gospels claim to present empirically valid accounts of Jesus' bodily disposition to speak and act as a free and authoritative agent. Through the testimony of Scripture there is a continuing and vital connection on the part of believers with the historic view of Jesus as incarnate person, from the time of his eye-witnesses to the period of Kant and the Enlightenment. In the Enlightenment, however, doubt about Jesus' claims arose through skeptical reinterpretation of the Gospels. Biblical authority was replaced by the authority of autonomous human reason.

In contrast, Strawson's analysis of persons and personhood as fundamentally social is a considerable aid to the exegesis of the Gospels and Jesus' role as creative agent. On the analogy of states of consciousness that are shared through bodily speech-acts in the public arena, we identify other persons as subjects of states of consciousness by their own particular bodily speech-acts.[29] Subjects cannot be identified as persons on the grounds of their unrevealed private states of consciousness, where there is only silence or staring. Consequently, the Cartesian ego can never be a proper subject for public discourse. That explains why the hermeneutics of Cartesian and Kantian dualism is destructive of the gospel data. It will not allow theological self-disclosure to occur in the realm of objective public fact and function propositionally and authoritatively as truth for all, everywhere and always. Dualism mandates that behavioral determinism reign supreme in the empirical domain of the sciences and history (naturalism), while freedom, value, and religious experience lie principally in the domain of private self-consciousness (subjectivism). This leads inevitably to a disincarnate, gnostic Christ, or to a humanized Jesus stripped of his messianic self-understanding. The hermeneutics of radical

[29]See Gruenler, *New Approaches*, 69–76.

gospel criticism does not allow Jesus' own states of consciousness and self-understanding to go public, except on the grounds of a humanized agenda preestablished by the subjective needs of the interpreter (e.g., existential, political, aesthetic).

Strawson describes how persons do in fact reveal themselves to one another, demonstrating that pure privatism and personhood are incompatible. Reality is social, and persons make themselves known by speaking and acting in the public sphere. Once that essential point is established, a more informed debate can be undertaken as to which speech-acts of Jesus will be acknowledged as authentically his own, and on what solid grounds one would reject the witness of the evangelists as historically suspect. In the final chapter it will be pointed out that Polanyi, in accord with Strawson's view of bodily enactment of personal disposition, maintains that knowing is always knowing in a social context of trust and commitment, and that where commitment and trust give way to suspicion and doubt, no one (indeed nothing) can be truly known as he really intends to be known, but becomes reinterpreted as a subjective concept in the private mind. This observation invites a serious reassessment of subjective idealistic hermeneutics and the skepticism that has seriously infected gospel interpretation since the Enlightenment.

It might also be noted that Strawson's definition of personhood as the psychophysical disclosure of the intentional self in a social context has its biblical counterpart at the archetypal level in the triune God, where the persons of the Trinity "embody" in the highest sense their dynamic and inexhaustible love and disposability toward one another in perfect social unity. This is the ultimate realism and the source of the real created world.[30] The triune God is accordingly the ultimate reality of "public personhood" and the archetypal Society, which creates a new society through the public work and words of the Son of God.

John R. Searle complements this common-sense analysis

---

[30]See Gruenler, *The Trinity in the Gospel of John.*

of embodied personal public language.[31] He continues the line of thought laid out by J. L. Austin and P. F. Strawson that speaking is not simply stating something with meaning but also doing something that gives the meaning force. Austin calls it the illocutionary or inferential act that attends the propositional locutionary utterance and results in perlocutionary effect. Searle contributes to the analysis of speech-acts by describing forms of behavior that aid the formulation of rules governing the various functions of speech-acts. It is important for our survey of his contribution to the hermeneutics of biblical interpretation to note that in his analysis the basic unit of communication is the speech-act, not the word or even the sentence. Hence good biblical exegesis must take account of the larger sense units of discoursing persons who are disclosed in the text. Exegesis should not focus solely on written pericopes or paragraphs in the Gospels and epistles but should also take account of those who generate and are revealed in the text. Someone said this, did this, or wrote this. That person is the ultimate referent of the textual discourse.

Accordingly, every proposition in the Scriptures must be seen contextually as having the backing of the one who is speaking authoritatively in a public setting and affords his audience clues as to the force of the statement he is making. The clues are in respect of the meaning he intends, how he intends it to count, and how he intends it to be taken. A speaker is effective in invoking these rules of expression if his discourse prepares an audience with a sincere promise and a willingly assumed obligation to perform a future act that underscores the point of the discourse. The object is an anticipated response on the part of the audience. The major functions of language, according to Searle's analysis, are telling others how things are, expressing our feelings and attitudes, committing ourselves to

---

[31]John R. Searle, *Speech Acts: An Essay in the Philosophy of Language* (London and New York: Cambridge University Press, 1969); idem, *Expression and Meaning: Studies in the Theory of Speech Acts* (London and New York: Cambridge University Press, 1979); John R. Searle and David Vanderveken, *Foundations of Illocutionary Logic* (Cambridge: Cambridge University Press, 1985).

appropriate acts, and bringing about changes by getting others to do things.[32] These would also describe the typical functions of Jesus' speech-acts, as well as the intended significance of speech-acts throughout Scripture.

The intended meaning of a speaker may of course be misunderstood or rejected by his audience and not bring about the intended result. Rejection or rebellion, rather than repentance and change, is often the audience response to the discourse acts of the prophets and Jesus. God's speech-acts in Scripture, however, always meet the conditions that Searle characterizes as successful illocutionary performance. The genuineness of discourse acts does not depend on pragmatic success in audience response, but on the fact that the conditions of successfully propounding something for consideration have been met: the speaker has spoken with clarity, with promise, and with genuine obligation to act on the truth of the stated proposition. God does without fail, Jesus does without fail: "For no matter how many promises God has made, they are 'Yes' in Christ" (2 Cor. 1:20; cf. 2 Sam. 22:31).

This brief survey of Strawson and Searle describes a larger school of language analysis that can be used with profit in analyzing various genres of illocutionary language in Scripture. With its aid, the exegete may better appreciate the varieties of propositional statements and their intended point and force within their proper settings in Scripture. The value of this methodology is that it compels the interpreter to recognize that religious statements, in all their generic variety, are propositions undersigned by persons who declare themselves and a certain state of affairs by speaking and acting in the public sphere of discourse. This is a method of descriptive realism, as distinguished from subjective idealism. In the latter, as we saw in part 1, religious language is primarily nonpropositional, private and subjective, not public or historical or factually normative, and it may even be assumed (as with Heidegger and the New

[32]Searle, *Expression and Meaning*, 29. See also Kevin J. Vanhoozer, "The Semantics of Biblical Literature: Truth and Scripture's Diverse Literary Forms," D. A. Carson and John D. Woodbridge, eds., *Hermeneutics, Authority, and Canon* (Grand Rapids: Zondervan, 1986), 87–91.

Hermeneutic) to have a life of its own, apart from persons who intend it, speak it, and enact it. A realistic reading of Scripture, however, will underscore the fact that God is personally intending, speaking, and enacting his Word with faithfulness and promise. He does this in the real and objective world of time-space and history, which he has created and imbued with meaning and which he sustains and employs as the vehicle of divine discourse. The subjective experience of discernment and trust comes only as a result of the objective disclosure and the acceptance of that disclosure. Subjective experience manifests itself objectively in the public sphere by commitment through specific speech-acts, such as public confession of faith, worship, proclamation of the gospel publicly in obedience to Christ, and holy deportment in the servant-image of Christ.

The Disclosure Function of Biblical Language: I. T. Ramsey. An especially creative philosopher in the functional analysis and logical empirical schools of British realism is Ian Ramsey, whose *Religious Language*[33] provides a valuable descriptive model as to how religious statements work in opening up situations of discernment where a proper commitment is made in response to divine disclosure. In mapping the logic of theological assertions Ramsey observes that the self-awareness of an agent like Jesus, who expresses himself in speech-acts, is not exhaustible by simple scientific verification. In the religious situation there is always something more than can be reduced to behavioral or causal factors, namely, the proclamation and recognition of a proposition of great consequence to which a free and total commitment is the proper response.

Such discernment-commitment situations are logically odd and ironic, since their meaning cannot be wholly discerned through ordinary logical and empirical testing. Yet they have a logic and an empirical verification of their own. For example, Jesus' enigmatic proposition, "Whoever wants to save his life will lose it, but whoever loses his life for me and for the gospel will save it" (Mark 8:35) is logically odd and untestable by

[33]I. T. Ramsey, *Religious Language: An Empirical Placing of Theological Phrases* (New York: Macmillan, 1963).

secular standards of verification but quite logical and testable in the larger empirical world of which Jesus is speaking and in which he is acting out paradigmatically his own servanthood. Ramsey effectively points out that the dimension of the logically odd in biblical language is actually an enlargement of logical and empirical knowing beyond the narrow limits of materialist and behavioral testing. From God's point of view, biblical language discloses that the real world is a world of value that encompasses every dimension of the logical world as well as the world of the empirical senses. It is in fact one world, and only a false idealism has separated the world into two unrelated compartments of fact and value (as in the varieties of Kantian dualism).

Indeed, as Ramsey observes, all knowing has a characteristically personal dimension in which a situation contains more than what is seen on the surface and takes on the character of vision, if it is to be truly understood. In coming to know Jesus through the gospel witnesses, the vision of understanding that grasps the significance of the person standing before us comes from discerning his person and mission and committing ourselves to him. Only then does the light shine, the ice break, and the penny drop. There are, of course, different levels of commitment required from different subjects and in various situations; commitment to another person is a deep and localized loyalty, while a commitment to mathematics is broad and universal. Ramsey describes the kind of commitment expected by Jesus as both deep and universal, since it is made to someone "from outside us," the Lord of the whole universe. Cosmic commitment to Christ is the highest function of language.

Jesus' use of the personal pronoun *I* is a significant factor in his assertion of his right to invite loyalty from his followers. Like Yahweh's "I AM WHO I AM" (Exod. 3:14), *I* is the irreducible tautology, the final posit, the apex word that says, "I say what I say and do what I do because I am I." Hence Jesus' language consists of final tautologies centering on his person and his use of the personal pronoun *I*, which sponsors key words and declares a divine commitment. His hearers either see or do not see the reality of divine disclosure standing in their midst, depending on their own discernment of and commitment to Jesus' bodily enactment of salvation. His authority in forgiving sins, stilling storms, feeding the hungry, healing the sick, exorcising demons, raising the dead, and proclaiming the good news of salvation and inaugurated eschatology enact the divine presence. His claims attest that he is speaking and acting with an odd yet recognizable kind of language designed to evoke a response of commitment among the discerning. Their discernment moves along a logical route until they see, at the end of the series, that Jesus completes and presides over the rest of human language. The language of the New Testament, enfolding the Old, is accordingly seen to center in the person of Jesus Christ, the "I am I," who may be pictured as the center of a maze, the spot where the committed finally arrive if they walk long enough in faith and make the correct logical moves. The claims of Jesus are therefore to be seen as a logical use of God-language, which is formed out of heightened ordinary models of experience, affording Jesus a distinctive placing and a presidential position over the whole language route.

Ramsey observes that because there is no single homogeneous scientific language and because we are at present puzzled as to what science is really about, it would be a mistake to assume that Scripture can be interpreted simply by separating fact from meaning. Facts are already complex and logically odd in ordinary situations and even more so in biblical situations, and they are full of meaning because God has already interpreted the facts by his act of creation. The miracle of the incarnation is a logically odd and riotous mixing of categories, as Word becomes flesh and dwells among us. To understand this odd language, just the right disclosure-commitment situation must be evoked. It is therefore the task of the interpreter to map the logical geography of divine disclosure in Scripture and to pay especial attention to the use of the personal pronoun *I* as it is used of God and the incarnate Christ in the speech-acts of revelation and redemption.

As Ramsey observes, the pronoun *I* is the best clue to all genuine mystery, all sublime paradox, and all revealing impropriety. While *I* is logically explorable, it is never logically exhaustible. Above all, it requires that one who plays the logical "game" be well experienced as a believer in the geography of the discernment-commitment situation.[34]

[34]For further discussion of Ramsey and the application of his methodology to New Testament exegesis, see Gruenler, *New Approaches*, 153–67.

6
AMERICAN SCHOOLS OF REALISM

In the 1970s a leading figure in the circles of New Testament liberal scholarship published an article that perceptively describes how the philosophy of religion took over the role of leadership from biblical studies in the Divinity School of the University of Chicago within a generation of its founding.[1] Robert Funk's case study is paradigmatic of the radical theological reorientation that could be documented of a large number of seminaries, colleges, and universities in America in the early years of the twentieth century. William R. Harper, a noted evangelical Old Testament scholar at Yale, had been invited to serve as president of the new University of Chicago in 1892. By the 1880s German biblical criticism had already seriously eroded confidence in the errancy of Scripture, and Harper undertook to meet German scholarship on its own terms by appointing a biblical faculty worthy of the challenge.

Harper's immediate appointment of Ernest DeWitt Burton as his New Testament counterpart proved, however, to have serious consequences and hastened the demise of biblical authority at Chicago. Burton, whose views on Scripture differed substantially from those of Harper, appointed Shailer Matthews to the department in 1894 and Shirley Jackson Case in 1908, both of whom were moving in distinctly liberal

[1]Robert Funk, "The Watershed of the American Biblical Tradition: The Chicago School, First Phase, 1892–1920," *JBL* 95 (1976): 4–22.

directions. Harper was dedicated both to a high view of biblical authority and to freedom of research and expression and tried to weave them together; but Burton separated critical interpretation from questions of hermeneutics and theology and treated it largely as a descriptive scientific discipline to be pursued in its own right. He underscored the role of history and social backgrounds, reversing Harper's orthodox biblical priorities and anticipating the liberal methodologies of Matthews and Case. Burton and his colleagues displaced Scripture to a secondary role by the rationalistic and naturalistic investigation of empirical data. By 1924, the date of Shailer Matthews' *Faith of Modernism*, the focus of authority at the Divinity School had long since shifted from Scripture to the scientific work of the historian, though Matthews still considered himself to be a man of the church. Shirley Jackson Case also gave priority to the historical method and developed a thoroughgoing social-contexts approach to the Bible. His criticisms were aimed at orthodox and liberals alike who were too much given, he felt, to a static analysis of historical documents. Critical biblical scholarship must be informed by the dynamic evolutionary nature of history. Christianity was a social process without normative character, a position he argued in *The Evolution of Early Christianity* (1914). It was only a matter of time before the Chicago school began to move into its second phase with the ascendancy of the philosophy of religion under Henry Nelson Wieman, Charles Hartshorne, and Bernard Meland. The biblical basis of faith had been effectively eroded within a generation; a university, with a biblical faculty at its core at the beginning, soon became a secular institution with no surviving evangelical witness.

Such has been the pervasive power of post-Enlightenment philosophy in institutions of higher learning in America (as in Europe and Britain) wherever belief in the authority of Scripture has been abandoned. While Funk would hardly claim to be an apologist for biblical inerrancy, he believes that even in other institutions where the transition from biblical to philosophical authority was not so swift as at Chicago and in the academic world at large there continues to be an antitheological bias and a systematic suppression of the question of Scripture just below the surface. It remains to be seen whether American liberal biblical scholarship will survive without addressing the hermeneutical question of authority and by continuing to trade on a sentiment it is not willing to acknowledge. The role of biblical studies in colleges and universities that no longer lay any claim to Judaeo-Christian roots is especially precarious in an increasingly pluralistic culture. Funk's own refusal to reopen the question of the authority of Scripture places him in the mainstream of liberal critical thought (he wants to accord full dignity to the ancient and honorable discipline of biblical interpretation without, as he says, a scriptural crutch). His counterproposal that perhaps biblical scholars should concern themselves with reviving their rich tradition under the guise of literary interpretation and the history of interpretation falls short of what is needed in the present crisis of the academy and the numerical decline within liberal seminaries and mainline denominations.

Are there strains of thought in American philosophy, especially within its schools of realism, that offer any promise to the biblical interpreter? An examination of the leading schools of American philosophical realism (pragmatism, critical realism, metaphysical realism) leads one to conclude that all are to one degree or another hostile to Scripture and supportive of human autonomy in the quest for meaning and significance. There is, however, a minority voice in the American tradition of philosophical realism that traces its heritage to the Reformation and Augustine by way of the Scriptures. This tradition promises more adequate resources for the hermeneutical quest than the philosophical schools examined thus far.

In the following pages we will examine the major secular schools of American realism and conclude with an exposition of a hermeneutical point of view that, in my opinion, is most comprehensive and faithful to Scripture. We will not consider American versions of idealism. While widely influential in our culture from early nineteenth-century Unitarianism through Emerson and Royce to the present, they have largely echoed

Continental idealisms that have already been considered and critiqued in part 1.

NATURALISTIC REALISM IN AMERICA

Mainstream American philosophy has in large part agreed with the Enlightenment dogma that meaning and understanding come by way of autonomous human reason working on sensory data, with little or no concern for the interpretation of reality afforded by Scripture. Charles Sanders Peirce (1839–1914) anticipated the practical pragmatism that was to become a distinctive way of life for secular Americans, a way of life based on belief in evolutionary process softened by a nominal gospel of love (the agapastic force, as he called it). For Peirce, God is hardly more than the influence some great character might have on human conduct. Scriptural revelation plays no role in his philosophical writings.[2]

It was William James (1842–1910) who developed Peirce's hermeneutical theories into the school of pragmatism by drawing on new research in psychology and the insights of British empiricists. For James the questions of traditional theology and philosophy concerning origins, principles, and

[2]See *The Collected Papers of Charles Sanders Peirce*, vols. 1–6, Charles Hartshorne and Paul Weiss, eds. (Cambridge: Harvard University Press, 1931–35); vols. 7–8, Arthur Burks, ed. (Cambridge: Harvard University Press, 1958). For a recent revival of Pierce and Royce and their naturalistic view of the community as the unifying matrix of pluralistic interpreters, see Robert S. Corrington, *The Community of Interpreters: On the Hermeneutics of Nature and the Bible in the American Philosophical Tradition*, Studies in American Biblical Hermeneutics 3 (Macon: Mercer University Press, 1987). Corrington rejects the hermeneutical approach that takes the Bible presuppositionally as an authoritative text and insists that the Bible must win its own way in the rhetorical terms and categories laid out by the culture (pp. vi–xviii). For a similar hermeneutical emphasis in liberal American Jewish exegesis, where "now" is normative, compare the remarks of Jacob Neusner, *Christian Faith and the Challenge of Judaism. The Judaic Encounter with Scripture* (Grand Rapids: Eerdmans, 1987): "What matters in Scripture is not the history of Scripture or even the historicity of the events portrayed in Scripture;" rather, the authority of Scripture "rests upon the community of the faithful today, not the events that . . . took place long ago" (p. xii).

categories were of little value. The new attitude of pragmatism looked to the practical results of behavior and of choosing actions and programs that would serve as instruments to achieve desired ends. Truth is defined as what works best in bringing personal happiness and organizing experiences successfully. True religion should not be concerned with revealed truth and doctrines but should serve to link the individual with an unseen larger life that produces the fruits of successful living. God is a higher but impersonal and finite part of a pluralistic universe.[3] James offers little to the biblical exegete in the way of useful methodology except as a negative reminder that true happiness is obtained only when God's gracious offer of salvation is taken account of in the pragmatic operation. Otherwise the pursuit of happiness on naturalistic grounds alone is short-sighted and short-lived and, according to Scripture, terminates in divine judgment.

Undoubtedly the most influential proponent of the school of pragmatism was John Dewey (1859–1952), whose realism was totally naturalistic and positivistic. Drawing from biology, psychology, and sociology, Dewey viewed the evolutionary adaptation of the mind to the real world as a practical attempt to gain mastery of the environment. Truth and values are constantly changing as human beings in society adapt to new conditions and work out practical formulas to achieve desired ends. Virtual truth is that plan of action that seems to promise a satisfactory result; terminal truth is achieved when the plan works. Dewey sometimes referred to this as a "religious attitude," but it had nothing to do with a personal God, Scripture, sin, salvation, or life everlasting.[4]

The religion of humanism in the philosophies of Peirce,

---

[3]See William James, *The Varieties of Religious Experience: A Study in Human Nature* (New York: Random House, n.d. [1902]); idem, *Essays in Radical Empiricism* and *A Pluralistic Universe* (New York: Longmans, Green, 1940 [1909]); idem, *Essays in Pragmatism* (New York: Hafner, 1948 [1907]).

[4]See John Dewey, *Reconstruction in Philosophy* (New York: Holt, Rinehart and Winston, 1920); idem, *The Quest for Certainty* (New York: Putnam, 1929); M. H. Thomas, ed., *John Dewey: A Centennial Bibliography* (Chicago: University of Chicago, 1962).

James, and Dewey emerges through a distinctive American fascination with practicality and is further articulated in the writings of the new realists, Ralph Barton Perry (1876–1957) and George Santayana (1863–1952). Perry, like Dewey, developed his humanistic faith around a hermeneutical commitment to naturalism and empiricism. The world is value-neutral, hence a liberal religion devoid of theological or metaphysical doctrine can aid the human achievement of higher values by opening up new possibilities.[5] The "critical realism" of Santayana claimed to meet a materialistic and mechanistic reality through reason combined with intuitive "animal faith," a prephilosophical grasp of what exists independently in the real world. Religion functions as myth and poetry in human imagination; combined with piety and spirituality, it produces rational religion.[6]

It can readily be seen that the predominant schools of realism indigenous to America at the turn of the century are hostile to revealed religion and contribute little to the quest for a sound philosophical framework for biblical hermeneutics. While claiming technically to be "realisms," they are in fact only variations on the theme of idealism, since the individual or community of individuals creates the ideal ends that are the goals of practical projects and of faith. No God or supreme personal intelligence discloses the nature of reality to the human mind.

METAPHYSICAL REALISM IN AMERICA

More recently, however, a school of metaphysical realism has emerged on American soil that continues to claim wide allegiance among liberal religious thinkers and has even begun to make inroads into evangelical thought. In chapter 5, British schools of realism were briefly considered and critiqued, among them the metaphysical realism of Alfred North Whitehead.

[5]Ralph Barton Perry, *Puritanism and Democracy* (New York, 1944); idem, *Realms of Value* (Cambridge: Harvard University, 1954).

[6]George Santayana, *Scepticism and Animal Faith* (New York: Dover, 1955 [1923]) idem, *Winds of Doctrine* (New York: Scribner, 1913).

Since Whitehead's major philosophical writings on realism were completed at Harvard University, where he moved from Britain in the twenties, and were continued by his American disciple Charles Hartshorne, it is important to reconsider the school as a significant option in the marketplace of competing contemporary American philosophical hermeneutics.

Whitehead's principal doctrines, it will be recalled, are as follows:[7]

1. Creativity (i.e., creative process) is the encompassing principle of all reality, to which God is supremely beholden.

2. God has two natures: (1) The primordial nature of God is pure unconscious and unrealized possibility which organizes possibilities to serve as lures for the creative evolutionary advance of the present actual universe. (2) The consequent nature of God describes the conscious aspect of God that receives data from the myriad free entities or "occasions" of the processing universe. As a consequence of receiving these experience-data, God becomes conscious and "alive," but he is necessarily finite and limited in his actuality, since he is confined to the process of time and space and does not know the future as it actually will be. Process is, by definition, advance into novelty, and God is supremely subject to it.

3. God cannot know the future as actual because the real world is "incurably atomic," i.e., creative freedom lies at the individual level of entities or occasions, and God does not know their decisions until they are made.

4. God has always had and will always have some universe or other because he necessarily needs the social data of actual occasions in order to be consequent and actual himself.

5. Accordingly, God is not sovereign over creation, has not brought it into being, and cannot prophetically disclose its future. Whitehead firmly rejects what he calls the "oriental despot" model of Judaism, Christianity, and Islam. Yet he holds to the hope that the lures of a limited God will lead toward the social "intensity of harmonious feeling" among the entities of the universe in its creative advance.

---

[7]From Whitehead's *Process and Reality*, his major work.

6. Whitehead's view of process and reality may therefore be understood to be essentially aesthetic rather than theological or ethical, since it is harmonious feeling rather than divine righteousness that guides the evolutionary advance.

7. Finally, as regards the self, Whitehead denies that any entity, including the individual human being, has a substantial nature. The human "occasion" (like all other occasions) becomes itself with respect to the process; it then peaks and perishes, without hope of conscious immortality.

Charles Hartshorne adopts Whitehead's focus on process and adds several variations of his own:[8]

1. Hartshorne defines God as divinely related or "relative" to everything in the universe (hence the title of his primary work, *The Divine Relativity*). But God is not related in the absolute sense of which Scripture speaks, i.e., as the sovereign Lord of creation. God is absolute only in a relative sense, since he does not oversee the immediate consciousness, freedom, or power of individual entities in the universe but receives their contributions only after they have made their decisions. God's Absoluteness (A) is therefore redefined as limited absoluteness. God functions something like the president of a democracy in the sense that he has to share power with independent entities throughout the universe. Since God is Relative (R) to all as lure to their creativity and as recipient of their self-created data, he is AR: i.e., Absolute in some respects but not all, and Related in some respects but not all.

2. Accordingly, God's relationship to the universe on a supreme level is analogous to the relationship of the mind to the body on the human level, in the sense that the universe constitutes God's "body." He is the dominant factor or "feeling" (or dominant monad, in Leibniz's terminology) in a

---

[8]See Charles Hartshorne, *The Divine Relativity: A Social Conception of God*, new ed. (New Haven: Yale University Press, 1964); idem, *The Logic of Perfection and Other Essays in Neoclassical Metaphysics* (La Salle, Ill.: Open Court, 1972). See also R. G. Gruenler, *The Inexhaustible God* (Grand Rapids: Baker, 1983), esp. chaps. 5, 6, for a longer review and critique of Whitehead's and Hartshorne's major theses; idem, "There and Back Again: A Journey in Process," in Ronald Nash, ed., *Process Thought* (Grand Rapids: Baker, 1987).

democracy of feelings that constitute the processing cosmic body; we are his brain cells. Hartshorne calls this "panentheism," since everything is in God. As the dominant consciousness of the universe, God attempts to persuade its constituent parts to exercise their relative freedom by making harmonious and beautiful choices. By making aesthetically positive choices, the cosmic body continues its quest of the never-ending goal of sociality in the evolutionary creative advance. The process will never be completed because of the resilience of selfishness and disharmony in the universe over which God has no ultimate sovereign control.

3. Hartshorne's realism is therefore dipolar, as God is dipolar. Part of reality has actualized and perished and is held in objective immortality in the memory of God. There is no subjective immortality, however, for no entity, not even a person, survives death. The other pole of "reality" is the as-yet-unactualized range of possibilities that lie in the future, from which God and the whole spectrum of free entities must make choices. According to the logic of process theism, these choices must be made in total isolation from each other, otherwise God and other emerging occasions would interfere with one another's freedom (the defense of human freedom is of paramount importance for the school).

In *The Inexhaustible God* I have critiqued both Whitehead and Hartshorne, along with other prominent advocates of process theism.[9] My principal reason for rejecting process realism as a workable hermeneutical tool for biblical interpretation is that the school uniformly dismisses the revelatory authority of Scripture. It adopts a Kantian epistemology in the place of Scripture, and this epistemology accords pride of place to speculative and autonomous human reason in the interpretation of empirical data. The fact that Kant was antimetaphysical and process thought is metaphysical makes little difference in

[9]E.g., Schubert Ogden, *The Reality of God* (New York: Harper & Row, 1966); John B. Cobb, Jr., *A Christian Natural Theology* (Philadelphia: Westminster, 1965); Lewis Ford, *The Lure of God: A Biblical Background for Process Theism* (Philadelphia: Fortress, 1978); Robert C. Neville, *Creativity and God: A Challenge to Process Theology* (New York: Seabury, 1980).

the outcome. Pivotal biblical teachings concerning God's sovereignty, creation, the Fall, human sin, redemption in Christ, resurrection, and eschatology are all dismissed or broadly reinterpreted. God has become a finite deity of limited power, defined largely in respect of aesthetics rather than righteousness and revealed in nature and human thought rather than in inspired and propositional Scripture.

There are serious logical problems in process theism's interpretation of reality:[10]

1. According to Hartshorne, God in his actuality is limited to space and time, yet he is able to encompass the entirety of the processing universe simultaneously at every moment. This is not an inconsiderable accomplishment if he is processing only at a finite velocity in time. The biblical God, on the other hand, can indeed do both, since he is both above time as sovereign creator of space-time and guarantor of all reality, and is within time in all its temporal sequences as sustainer, judge, and redeemer.[11]

2. According to process philosophy, the self has no substantiality in its procession and thus (as in Buddhism) presents an enigma as to the identity of the personal *I* from birth to death. An even greater enigma is how in the process system God's *I* has any substantiality independent of the processing universe that gives it content.

3. According to the process school, the social nature of God is not to be found in the relationship of the Trinity prior to and independent of creation, but only with respect to the cosmos itself. The entities of the universe are necessary to God if he is to have social experience. Hence God is contingent, that is, he is finite and dependent on something other than himself. This requires an unresolved and therefore everlasting dualism, a new version of ancient Zoroastrianism.

4. Redemption is self-redemption through the exercise of aesthetic choices. No savior is needed, only divine lure and

---

[10]For a detailed critique, see Gruenler, *The Inexhaustible God.*

[11]See esp. chap. 4, "Process and Simultaneity in God," ibid., for an extensive discussion of the logical difficulties in the process view of time.

direction for the self-actualizing entity. Hence Scripture is largely mythological in its views of the Fall, sin, eternal punishment, atonement, resurrection, and everlasting life.

In sum, there are too many presuppositions in process theism that are foreign to biblical revelation for it to serve substantially as a hermeneutical framework for the exegesis of Scripture. As noted before, however, one point at which the school has had a lasting and illuminating effect on the present writer is in its emphasis on the social nature of reality. Although it wrongly sees God's sociality as necessarily bound to some independent universe everlastingly, the social concept is fundamentally sound and biblical. Approaching the Gospel of John with a hermeneutical appreciation of the social nature of God, for example, the interpreter is able to see how Jesus discloses a societal theme in his dialogues with the Father and in his description of the work of the Holy Spirit in concert with Father and Son.[12] Moreover, the societal nature of God is a theme that runs throughout the Old and New Testaments and offers ethical directions for the people of God and their stewardship over the house of nature.[13] Process theism therefore suggests an important focus for biblical exegesis; but it is too committed to a speculative and autonomous defense of human freedom to be of greater value in fashioning a broad philosophical base for biblical interpretation. For that, it is necessary to turn elsewhere.

In the next section of this chapter we will examine in a preliminary and programmatic manner a rich, if minority, opinion in American philosophical-theological thought that is pertinent to our search. We will combine this with the substantial clues already gathered from some of the British realists (chapter 5), adding in the process some reflections of our own.

---

[12]See R. G. Gruenler, *The Trinity in the Gospel of John* (Grand Rapids: Baker, 1986).

[13]These themes are to be articulated in future publications by the author.

TOWARD A NEW ARTICULATION OF BIBLICAL REALISM

One of the early and most notable native American philosopher-theologians, Jonathan Edwards (1703–1758), combined a number of philosophical strands in his imaginative hermeneutics. Dedicated to a high view of Scripture and an Augustinian-Calvinist worldview, he adopted a metaphysical realism similar to Augustine's, which utilized Platonic idealism informed by biblical revelation (the most substantial things are not material but spiritual). Edwards acknowledged that the active mind functions in matters of choice and feeling yet at the same time is guided by divinely given principles such as being, cause, finality, and the like. In this regard he anticipated and preempted Kant by rejecting the autonomy of experience and reason, the latter being a fault of many of America's prominent thinkers during and following the Enlightenment. From Locke's *Essay on Human Understanding* (see chapter 1 of our study) he gained an appreciation of empiricism without succumbing to Locke's dismissal of innate ideas. He combined ardent Christian mystical piety with a conceptual view of the objective reality of God and his creation. He considered Scripture to be the highest revelation of God and the source of knowledge about salvation. Salvation in Christ brings about a transformation of the mind through the presence of the Holy Spirit, affording a new worldview of God's reality and the promise of eternal life. In Edward's writings one finds an indigenous American expression of the glorious sovereignty of God and of human responsibility in a real world that is known through general revelation and the Spirit's special revelation in the Scriptures.[14]

In the quest of a thoroughly biblical hermeneutical worldview, it was a remarkable group of American thinkers in the Augustinian-Reformed tradition who led the way. B. B. Warfield (1851–1921) is especially notable as one of America's most imaginative and scholarly philosopher-theologians who

[14]See Jonathan Edwards, *A Treatise on the Religious Affections* in *The Works of Jonathan Edwards*, ed. E. Hickman (Edinburgh: Banner of Truth, 1974).

faithfully exposited biblical realism. God creates, sustains, and interprets creation, constantly maintaining human beings in their rational and empirical relationships to the external world. The world is not a creation of the human mind, nor of blind chance for all rational and sensory knowledge is the result of God's continual interpreting presence in creation. Knowledge that saves comes from the Scriptures, for they bear witness to the true light who is Christ.[15] Because of God's revelation of himself in nature through common grace and through Scripture by special grace, points of contact with God (univocality) are established in creation and in the human heart and mind, which make possible the understanding of God, man, and the world and the sinner's return home.

It is on the basis of this Augustinian-Reformed tradition, held by notable contemporary philosophical-theological thinkers like Carl F. H. Henry, Gordon H. Clark, and Cornelius Van Til, among others, that a new appreciation of biblical realism is being expressed for the present generation.[16] Discerning criticism of the Kantian hermeneutical model is common to the school, as is a creative and faithful representation of scriptural evidence for belief that God is the author of all genuine knowledge and is the only guarantor of objective truth and certainty. The articulation of Augustinian-Reformed realism for our time should flow beyond geographical and ethnic lines that have distinguished the peculiar contributions of Western secular philosophical schools described in our study. The valuable insights of both idealism and realism may be gathered up and returned to their Author, who creates, upholds, and interprets the universe continuously by his word of power. In articulating a philosophical worldview that is solidly based on scriptural revelation and includes hermeneutical principles garnered from the Augustinian-Reformation tradition and its modern interpreters, the following points will invite serious consideration:

---

[15]B. B. Warfield, *The Inspiration and Authority of the Bible* (Philadelphia: Presbyterian and Reformed, 1964); idem, *Studies in Tertullian and Augustine* (New York: Oxford University Press, 1930).

[16]For bibliography, see For Further Reading.

1. The human search for meaning and understanding is "a consultation of God." Since God has left his imprint on everything he has made and has created persons in his own image, enabling them (insofar as they are enabled) to think his thoughts after him and to fellowship with him, he is the true light that enlightens every one who is born (John 1:9).[17]

2. God transcends the universe as creator and is not to be identified pantheistically with the world or with human thought. Intuition of the structures of meaning and symmetry that God has placed in the world is mediated by God as he continually reflects the thoughts of his own mind into human understanding. Whether humans recognize it or not, they are constantly dependent on God for the intricate network of life and meaning that sustains them ecologically, intellectually, and spiritually.

3. Since all meaning and significance on every level of creation is sustained by God's continuing general revelation, persons can be assured of the objective reality of truth. Truth is objectively "there" to be discovered because God, the author and guarantor of truth, places his signature on everything he creates. Everything belongs to him, refers to him, and has its objectivity in him who is the faithful creator and sustainer (Rom. 1:20).

4. Human rebellion against God's sovereign interpretation of his creation has radically defaced the noetic ability of human beings to interpret creation correctly or to live ethically according to the principles indelibly inscribed on it by God. As a consequence of sin God has subjected the creation to futility, but he has also subjected it to hope by his grace (Rom. 8:20). All human knowledge therefore leads ultimately to misinterpretation and death if one remains unredeemed, but leads to truth and eternal life if one undergoes repentance toward God in mind and will through faith in Jesus Christ (Acts 20:21).

[17]As Michael Polanyi has remarked, "the process of examining any topic is both an exploration of the topic, and an exegesis of our fundamental beliefs in the light of which we approach it; a dialectical combination of exploration and exegesis." *Personal Knowledge: Towards a Post-Critical Philosophy*, (New York: Harper & Row, 1964), 267.

Through the revelation of truth in the Scriptures, attested by the Holy Spirit in the act of regeneration, believers are released from the suppression of redemptive truth imaged in creation and from the bondage of a disobedient will, to thank God, glorify him, and ascribe all knowledge, all meaning, and all significance to him. The perfection of this inaugurated transformation in meaning and understanding is eschatological and awaits the final revelation at the end of the age, when we shall no longer "see . . . a poor reflection as in a mirror; then we shall see face to face," and "shall know fully" just as we are "fully known" (1 Cor. 13:12).

5. All knowledge is therefore revelational. To know anything is to that extent to know God the revealer and interpreter. Such is Calvin's view in the opening of the *Institutes*.[18] Since God continually reveals himself in all that he has made, all knowledge is co-knowledge, i.e., knowledge is the consultation of God's mind as he discloses himself in creation. Knowledge of the self is at the same time knowledge of God, since God has indelibly written his signature on human life, as on everything in his created universe. All belongs to him and refers to him. All knowledge is therefore referential to God, who is the ultimate Reality.

6. All knowledge is given to human beings primarily for the purpose of fostering personal and moral faithfulness in creative social relationship with the personally social God. It is given secondarily with his extensively interrelated and social creation. All meaning and significance, all proper hermeneutical method and genuine knowledge are fundamentally social because they derive from the dynamic and inexhaustible social nature of the triune God.

7. Conjectural philosophy, which derives from the autonomous speculations of the fallen human heart cannot be the source of true knowledge, as Scripture attests (1 Cor. 1:18–25; Col. 2:8). In the presence of genuine repentance and "faith

[18]John Calvin, *Institutes of the Christian Religion*, 2 vols. (Philadelphia: Westminster, 1960), I, 2, 1. A return to biblical realism might be signaled by the theme, "Beyond Kant to Calvin."

seeking understanding," revelational theology that is grounded in the person and work of Christ confirms God's objective revelation of himself throughout creation and affirms a true love of wisdom ("philosophy" in the highest sense). The problem of knowledge (philosophically speaking, the epistemological problem) does not lie in the inaccessibility of "things in themselves," as Kantian idealism asserts, since the facts of creation objectively "show and tell" in God's continual disclosure of truth through general revelation. The attributes of God himself are disclosed in creation and are clearly perceived deep within the human mind, sufficient to render humanity without excuse before the divine tribunal. The source of the epistemological and hermeneutical problem lies rather in the perverse rebellion of the human will, which demands the right to interpret all meaning and significance on its own terms, apart from the sovereign hermeneutics of God. Paul succinctly describes this great and terrible exchange of the glory of God for foolishness as a wicked suppression of truth that invites divine wrath (Rom. 1:18–23).

8. Ignorance of the real world and the real God cannot therefore be claimed by any human being as an excuse from responsibility. Humanity has deep within it noetic knowledge of God and of his objective creation. Everything attests God's power, righteousness, and grace, from scientific analysis to philosophical reasoning. Hence the value of persistent logical pressure, like Alvin Plantinga's insistence that the ontological argument for the existence of God has never received a cogent and conclusive refutation because there is nothing contrary to reason in the argument.[19] The Society of Christian Philosophers assumes the cogency of Christianity in the marketplace of philosophy, as does the correlative work of the American Scientific Affiliation in its creative integration of science and Christianity.

9. Christianity is therefore consummately rational, if indeed "logically odd" to the fallen human mind, which always

[19]Alvin Plantinga, *The Ontological Argument: From St. Anselm to Contemporary Philosophers* (Garden City, N.Y.: Doubleday, 1965); idem, *God and Other Minds: A Study of the Rational Justification of the Belief in God* (Ithaca: Cornell University Press, 1967).

embraces irrationalism at the end of the road in order to defend its autonomy. Christian faith provides ultimate meaning and significance because it is grounded in God's objective and authoritative disclosures in nature and in the redemptive work of Jesus Christ, attested by the witness of the Spirit in trustworthy Scripture. It is the claim of Christ and his witnesses that his saving work on the cross and in his resurrection extends to all an opportunity to exchange the presupposition of rebellion and unbelief for the presupposition of belief in the God who graciously creates, sustains, reveals, and redeems.

10. The philosophical framework for biblical interpretation must therefore find its foundation in Scripture, where things that are skewed are set right and plumb lines are established for the building of the house of knowledge. Once that foundation is in place, and the walls are erected perpendicularly, guidelines may be applied discerningly to available philosophical systems as to their usability in finishing the work of the building. Selections from these philosophies, depending on their faithfulness to God's general and special disclosures in creation and Scripture, may be made by biblical interpreters when imaginative insights into God's reality, or intuitions of his glorious handiwork, come to light.

Much remains to be done. The Scriptures have not revealed their last profound truth, as faithful and persistent exegetes regularly discover. Nor has God spoken his last word in his vast creation, where he provides for his creatures and continues to disclose awesome beauty, power, and complex symmetry. The real and objective world, which the Lord upholds by his word of power, has many secrets yet to reveal. If these truths can be sought in the spirit of faith seeking understanding, with a desire to thank, praise, and glorify God, it may well be that our generation will find new heuristic impulses of genuine discovery in the world where God continually speaks and acts, and these may aid our interpretation of Scripture. But we sorely need the gift of discernment (1 Cor. 12:10) in order to "test the spirits to see whether they are from God" (1 John 4:1).

Every philosophy, no matter how distorted, contains

some element of truth, for God has not left himself without witness in the world. The image of God, however suppressed, is imprinted deep within the human heart and mind. Yet as we have seen in our study of modern philosophies stemming from the Renaissance and the Enlightenment, the repudiation of special revelation in the Scriptures has been so permeating and so persistent that the biblical interpreter must constantly be alert. When faith in Christ as Savior and Lord is uppermost and God's special revelation in Scripture is allowed to transform one's view of the world, the interpreter becomes trained to discern and appreciate discoveries of God's truth wherever they may appear.

Accordingly, it is the mode of "faith seeking understanding" that provides the means of thinking God's thoughts after him and of acquiring knowledge of his creation. God's wisdom is built into the universe because he who has created it is wisdom personified. Hence the quest for wisdom, meaning, and understanding is a legitimate and necessary pursuit. Christian philosophers should play a significant role in the interpretive process by providing important hermeneutical skills and insights in the use of logic, reasoning, analysis of presuppositions, ethics, aesthetics, and the weighing of world-views.

The inspired writers of the Old and New Testament Scriptures made use of thought patterns in their cultures that reflected the general revelation of God in nature and history and transformed and purified them by the leading of the Spirit.[20] When the fullness of time had come and the setting was right, God sent forth his Son (Gal. 4:4). It is not too much to hope that in our own time, when the complexities of God's creation are being revealed on an ever-increasing cosmic scale, Christian philosophers will work hand in hand with biblical interpreters and theologians (and with others in related fields of inquiry) to strengthen the hermeneutical foundations for sound exegesis of Scripture and to aid in the application of its truths to the

---

[20]See, e.g., Meredith G. Kline, *Treaty of the Great King* (Grand Rapids: Eerdmans, 1963).

gracious and fragile house we live in, as good stewards of our Lord's creation and of his Word, until he comes back to complete what he has begun.

7

BIBLICAL APPLICATION: THE AUGUSTINIAN REALISM OF MICHAEL POLANYI

One of the most perceptive of twentieth-century philosophers in the field of epistemology and hermeneutics was the expatriate Hungarian scientist, sociologist, and philosopher Michael Polanyi (1891–1976), whose major philosophical work was undertaken with deep appreciation of the democratic climate of Britain and the democracies in the West. Some of the finest writing on hermeneutics in this century will be found in the central chapters of his epochal study, *Personal Knowledge: Towards a Post-Critical Philosophy*.[1] All too aware of the tragic consequences of modern tyrannical idealist political philosophies on the Continent and concerned about ridding the scientific community of its dogmatic cult of objectivity, Polanyi writes with great sensitivity and often with incisive brilliance on hermeneutical questions. He describes how persons come to know what they know: by "faith seeking understanding," the venerable Augustinian formula.

The process of knowing is made possible, he argues, by a tacit awareness of an objective reality that discloses itself in the commitment situation. Although he was himself a scientist,

[1]Michael Polanyi, *Personal Knowledge: Towards a Post-Critical Philosophy* (New York: Harper & Row, 1964), 5. First published in 1958, the work is based on Polanyi's Gifford Lectures, 1951–52, delivered in the University of Aberdeen and dedicated to Principal Sir Thomas and Lady Taylor, prominent Christian leaders in the Church of Scotland.

Polanyi rejects the ideal of impersonal scientific detachment and follows an alternative ideal of knowledge based on action that is accomplished by skills of which we are only tacitly or subsidiarily aware and which are learned in trust. When we focus on doing something (say, a project in biblical exegesis) and attend *to* this project, we tacitly attend *from* clues and skills that are not observed but tacitly used. In every undertaking, "we can know more than we can tell and we can tell nothing without relying on our awareness of things we may not be able to tell."[2] Things we can tell we know by observation, and those we cannot tell we know by indwelling them with personal commitment in the fiduciary mode of belief and trust. The latter is fundamental to the first; hence tacit or subsidiary knowing is more basic than explicit or focal knowing and provides the heuristic basis for all new discovery.

While Polanyi adopts less than persuasive views on issues somewhat tangential to his major contribution (though not inconsequential for the evangelical: his theology is sometimes fuzzily Tillichian and dated [he is neither a biblical exegete nor a theologian], his views on emergent evolution are naïvely optimistic, and his professed similarity to Heidegger's philosophy of being-in-the-world is somewhat strained), he is brilliant in his analysis of modern doubt and equally impressive in describing how human knowledge rests on tacit belief in the reality of an objective world, within an affirming community (as Christians have always held). His fundamental hermeneutical principle is that "into every act of knowing there enters a passionate contribution of the person knowing what is being known, and that this coefficient is no mere imperfection but a vital component of his knowledge."[3] A neo-Augustinian-Platonist, Polanyi contends that there is objective truth and rationality to reality that is not only tacitly presupposed by scientists but "trains" us (whether we are aware of it or not) to recognize its inner qualities. Scientific achievement, including the science

---

[2]Polanyi, *Personal Knowledge*, x. See also idem, *The Tacit Dimension* (New York: Doubleday, 1966), 3–25.

[3]Polanyi, *Personal Knowledge*, xiv.

of biblical interpretation, always proceeds from an "intuition" of rationality in the object of research, and this intuition precedes empirical verification. This corroborates the Augustinian principle of "faith seeking understanding" (*fides quaerens intellectum*). Scientific methodology begins with tacit belief in the objective world (the fiduciary mode at the subsidiary level), then proceeds to the testing of a hypothesis (the fiduciary mode at the focal level). The combination of the fiduciary and the intuitional overcomes the purely relativistic pragmatism of positivism, which Polanyi sees as a serious threat to the stability of Western culture.

Because of the fiduciary nature of all knowing in both its tacit and focal components, Polanyi warns that his purpose "is to show that complete objectivity as usually attributed to the exact sciences is a delusion and is in fact a false ideal."[4] No theory can be relieved of the scientist's personal conforming judgment as long as that theory is held to be true. Acts of personal judgment form an essential part of the sciences (and of the sciences associated with biblical criticism, as we have seen throughout our study). This does not of course ascribe a purely subjective value to the research of scientist-scholars, since we assume the universal validity of our appraisals of reality and tacitly assume that we are making true statements about likely events.[5] All meaning and significance are underwritten by my personal faith that this is the case, universally. It is by my *personal* appraisal that *I believe* what a sentence says.[6]

The strength of Polanyi's epistemology comes to clearest expression in his analysis of acquiring skills. Applying his description of skills to gospel interpretation, we may come to appreciate in a new way that what Jesus is announcing cannot be learned only in precept but must also and especially be learned by example and imitation of that example by faith and the practice of the art of discipleship. In the art of Jesus' teaching and acting out the skills of discipleship, the believer discovers

[4]Ibid., 18.
[5]Ibid., 22–25.
[6]Ibid., 25.

the faith and skills that eventually flower and bear fruit (e.g., in the context of the footwashing: "A new command I give you: Love one another. As I have loved you, so you must love one another. By this all men will know that you are my disciples, if you love one another" (John 13:34–35). Such art can be passed on only from master to apprentice-disciple, since there is no precise prescription for such unspecifiable art. Here a comparison could be made between the gospel and its interpreters and between Jesus and his disciples, where Jesus is the master teacher and the interpreter is the apprenticed disciple. "To learn by example is to submit to authority," says Polanyi:

> You follow your master because you trust his manner of doing things even when you cannot analyze and account in detail for its effectiveness. By watching the master and emulating his efforts in the presence of his example, the apprentice unconsciously picks up the rules of the art, including those which are not explicitly known to the master himself. These hidden rules can be assimilated only by a person who surrenders himself to that extent uncritically to the imitation of another. A society which wants to preserve a fund of personal knowledge must submit to tradition.[7]

That is an important passage for the gospel interpreter. Applied to biblical exegesis, Polanyi's hermeneutical analysis implies obedience to the text of authoritative Scripture and an attentiveness to the art of Jesus the master teacher, whose skill consists of the unspecifiable art of servanthood on behalf of the sinner, the poor, the sick, the oppressed, the widow, and the orphan and of his willingness to die for the lost. A genuine understanding of Jesus in the Gospels does not come from some neutral objective and uncommitted position assumed apart from discipleship, but only from obedience to the master teacher who exercises skills of discipleship to a consummate degree. With practice these develop into master skills, or "connoisseurship": "Connoisseurship, like skill, can be communicated only by

[7]Ibid., 53.

example, not by precept; . . . you must go through a long course of experience under the guidance of a master."[8]

In the practice of attentiveness and obedience an apprentice gradually develops two kinds of awareness, one a subsidiary or distal awareness, which transposes one from knowing what to knowing how (the tacit component of thought and action), and the other a focal or proximal awareness, which is the application of the skill or connoisseurship to the practical needs at hand. The good New Testament interpreter will increasingly speak and act with a genuine transparency to the gospel language of which he or she is tacitly aware in personal commitment. That is, one indwells a certain set of presuppositions, just as one indwells one's body.[9] The guiding principle in gospel interpretation, as in the exegesis of all the Scriptures, thus becomes an openness and commitment to the One who confronts and invites the disciple to follow him. True knowledge of the Jesus of the Gospels comes only through commitment to him and by practicing his art. Apprenticeship and connoisseurship require an element of passivity and trust, of discovery and submission, of feelings one's way in humble obedience. One lives in it as in the garment of one's own skin:

> The act of personal knowing can sustain these relations only because the acting persons believes . . . that he has not *made them* but *discovered them*. The effort of knowing is thus guided by a sense of obligation towards the truth: by an effort to submit to reality.[10]

In describing the grammar of the tacit component, Polanyi illustrates how important a limited language is for finite human beings, and how important is its repeated usage and consistency. The first he calls the law of poverty, pointing out that from an alphabet of twenty-three letters we could conceiv-

---

[8]Ibid., 54.

[9]Ibid., 60. Compare this approach with that of Cornelius Van Til, who is also a presuppositionalist. See Van Til's introduction in B. B. Warfield, *The Inspiration and Authority of the Bible* (Philadelphia: Presbyterian and Reformed, 1948), 3–68, esp. 68.

[10]Polanyi, *Personal Knowledge*, 63. His emphasis.

ably construct 23^8, that is, about one hundred thousand million eight-letter code words. Each sentence could thus be replaced by a different word. But this would mean the destruction of language, although it would mean its millionfold enrichment, for no one could possibly remember all the code words. The relatively simple repetition of a few words and their associated actions makes language meaningful. It also makes the language of Jesus and the Gospels, as well as the Old Testament and epistolary genres, possible. From the law of poverty "it follows that a language must be poor enough to allow the same words to be used a sufficient number of times."[11] Paul's description of Christ, ". . . that though he was rich, yet for your sakes he became poor, so that you through his poverty might become rich" (2 Cor. 8:9) has implications that are far-reaching, not least regarding the poverty of expression by which Jesus communicates divine grace, and the poverty of action by which he evidences redemptive servanthood. Complementing the laws of poverty and grammar are the laws of iteration and consistency, where the repeatability of speech with consistent action makes the language-game understandable and manageable (hence the additional law of manageability).[12] Jesus' speech-acts in the Gospels contain a tacit component of simplicity and unspecifiability, requiring obedient apprenticeship if the disciple-interpreter is really to understand the Master, learn his art of servanthood, and pass it on.

Polanyi observes that in the use of ordinary scientific language, from the descriptive sciences to the exact sciences to the deductive sciences, there is a sequence of increasing formalization and symbolic manipulation and a decreasing contact with experience.[13] Applying this to biblical criticism, we find that the more the gospel material is analyzed without a sympathetic personal commitment to the central figure in the gospel story and to the reliability of the disciples whose eyewitness reportage lies behind the gospel texts, the more

[11]Ibid., 78.
[12]Ibid., 81.
[13]Ibid., 86.

abstract become the theories adduced to explain the development and redaction of the sayings and acts of Jesus, so that every step toward the behavioral ideal of causal reduction is achieved by a progressive sacrifice of content. This has been the history of radical criticism since the Enlightenment. Jesus has been interpreted in light of transitory cultural ideals rather than by the intrinsic claims of the gospel texts. The constructed portraits of Jesus in one generation are then deconstructed by the criticism of the next generation of scholars and replaced by new portraits (the Jesus of existential decision is now giving way to the Jesus of political liberation). Gospel interpretation that is based on the art of discipleship and listens obediently to the Gospels' witness will not be tempted to reconstruct them according to idealistic and naturalistic evolutionary theories. Increasingly one finds lay believers rejecting radical approaches to the Gospels. Moreover, a growing number of New Testament scholars are coming to appreciate that critical methods of analysis can be used positively or destructively, from within the story or outside it, and that a fiduciary commitment or lack of commitment to the principal figure of the Gospels determines the outcome of one's exegesis.

Polanyi warns that we deceive ourselves if we think that we can achieve truth by approaching an object of study (such as the Scriptures) in a spirit of critical doubt and "scientific" objectivism. No such impersonal objectivity and precision is to be found. Polanyi cites Kurt Gödel's important mathematical discovery of the early thirties to illustrate that the scope of mathematics, the basis of science, is indeterminate and cannot function without fiduciary commitment to its ultimate validity.[14] Every mathematical system assumes one's tacit trust in some higher metasystem. This is true with biblical criticism generally and gospel criticism in particular. If one is skeptical of the truth-claims of the evangelists that Jesus actually said and did what they report, one reveals not so much the truth about Jesus as one's tacit commitments about what is possible in history and what one wants to believe. The tacit beliefs of

[14]Ibid., 94, 118, 259.

radical critics do not share common ground with the commitments of Jesus and the evangelists, but are influenced by modern assumptions as to what is possible in a closed universe where the supernatural and the logically odd are ruled out. (An analysis of the intentions and assumptions that compel radical critics to deconstruct the Gospels would prove an interesting study.)

A characteristic attitude of humility is evident in Polanyi's epistemology when he acknowledges the risk and commitment that are tacitly required in every field of knowing. Understanding an object of study exhaustively is an unrealizable ideal, for neutral objectivity is impossible. Moreover, the object discloses itself only to the attentive and obedient beholder who approaches it with heuristic expectation; hence the unspecifiability of knowing, which rests on personal commitment to the validity of our quest for knowledge:

> For just as, owing to the ultimately tacit character of all our knowledge, we remain ever unable to say all that we know, so also, in view of the tacit character of meaning, we can never quite know what is implied in what we say.[15]

When this observation is applied to the gospel material and is not made to focus on some assumed conspiracy of the evangelists to fashion an altogether human Jesus into a supernatural Messiah but allows the Gospels to make their own case, then Jesus may make his claim on the reader and the critic. In this heuristic approach to the Gospels, Polanyi's general words take on special meaning:

> We have seen already that whenever we make (or believe we have made) contact with reality, we anticipate an indeterminate range of unexpected future confirmations of our knowledge derived from this contact.[16]

In Jesus' setting, where we have incarnate "genius," the contact with reality is on an extraordinarily wide range and of

[15]Ibid., 95.
[16]Ibid., 124.

deep intensity. The following passage is helpful in describing what Jesus' self-disclosure brings to light:

> Moreover, by deploying such powers in an exceptional measure—far surpassing ours who are looking on—the work of a genius offers us a massive demonstration of a creativity which can neither be explained in other terms, nor taken unquestioningly for granted. By paying respect to another person's judgment as superior to our own, we emphatically acknowledge originality in the sense of a performance the procedure of which we cannot specify. Confrontation with genius thus forces us to acknowledge the originative power of life, which we may and commonly do neglect in its ubiquitous lesser manifestations.[17]

This is applicable to the self-disclosure of Jesus. Receiving a disclosure requires the interpreter to experience something like an "ecstatic vision." It is not enough simply to be guided by experience and to pass through experience. The disclosure needs to be experienced in itself; and since the self-disclosure of Jesus is inseparable from the person who stands back of it, it is Jesus himself who is experienced through his very words and acts. Experiencing Jesus as he is portrayed in the Gospels requires an intellectual passion of "contemplation," which "dissolves the screen" of a manipulative conceptual framework,

> stops our movement through experience and pours us straight into experience; we cease to handle things and become immersed in them. Contemplation has no ulterior intention or ulterior meaning; in it we cease to deal with things and become absorbed in the inherent quality of our experience, for its own sake.[18]

Polanyi interprets this indwelling as something akin to Christian contemplation, like the communion of the Christian mystic and his experience of redemption. There is a joy, but a joy mixed with guilt and mounting tension in the ritual of worship, which moves from anguish to surrender to hope. Following this train of thought, access to the Jesus of the Gospels must be sought in the bracketing of conceptual prejudices and in surrender to the redeeming grace he offers:

[17]Ibid.

[18]Ibid., 197.

> It is man's surrender to the love of God, in the hope of gaining His forgiveness, and admission to His presence. The radical anti-intellectualism of the *via negativa* expresses the effort to break out of our normal conceptual framework and "become like little children." It is akin to the reliance on the "foolishness of God," that short-cut to the understanding of Christianity, of which St. Augustine said enviously that it was free to the simple-minded but impassable to the learned.[19]

Jesus is not authentically "observed," therefore, by the critic who makes a sustained effort of breaking out. Jesus is met only by one who shows love and desire for the holy and divine by breaking in:

> Proximity to God is not an observation, for it overwhelms and pervades the worshiper. An observer must be relatively detached from that which he observes, and religious experience transforms the worshiper. It stands in this respect closer to sensual abandon than to exact observation.[20]

Strong advice for the scientific historian and critic, yet a necessary antidote to the kind of gospel criticism that observes and handles and uses, but misunderstands because it stands outside the story. Polanyi fearlessly assails the opaque dogmas and prejudices of the modern critical mind. The proper approach to knowledge is not even like the indwelling of a great theory or like immersion in a musical masterpiece, "but the heuristic upsurge which strives to break through the accepted frameworks of thought, guided by the intimations of discoveries still beyond our horizon. . . ." This is especially true of the Gospels: "Christianity sedulously fosters, and in a sense permanently satisfies, man's craving for mental dissatisfaction by offering him the comfort of a crucified God."[21] In contrast, the modern alternative to the Christian model of contemplation focuses on an atomized and depersonalized universe in which everything at last becomes absurd and hostile, fragmented, and

[19]Ibid., 198.
[20]Ibid.
[21]Ibid., 199.

full of despair.[22] The radical doubt of our age has carried over into biblical studies, but only because of hermeneutical methods based on a mistaken notion of the scientific enterprise.

That having been said, it is to be noted that a hermeneutical approach that will bring the interpreter into an authentic meeting with Jesus will not come primarily from individual efforts of the scholar in isolation but within the conviviality of the believing community where the mind and the heart are apprenticed by master believers and interpreters. Such is the implication of Polanyi's next discourse—"Conviviality."[23] This point of view is shared by a number of biblical scholars and theologians who are beginning to appreciate again the inseparability of biblical scholarship and the believing community. The secular academic setting is not sufficient for the work of apprenticing interpreters of the Word. While it provides the principal means of conviviality for many other disciplines, the reigning attitude in most academic quarters of learning today is secular and positivisitic. Hence the milieu of conviviality afforded by the secular university will be largely hostile to the peculiar content of Scripture. The biblical scholar takes many professional risks if he maintains the integrity and historicity of contested Old Testament documents, the Gospels, the Pauline epistles, and the Book of Acts in such a setting, as many will attest. The tacit assumptions of positivism intimidate all but the hardiest, and little creative conviviality is possible on the central and most meaningful issues of Scripture, though professional research in the outer circles of less contested data (e.g., background and linguistic studies) can often be convivial and productive.

Accordingly, biblical interpretation that is faithful to the divine Author and witnessing authors of Scripture will be nurtured principally in the believing community as it flows from older to younger, and from mature believer to novice:

> This assimilation of great systems of articulate lore by novices of various grades is made possible only by a *previous act of affiliation,*

---

[22]Ibid., 200.

[23]Ibid., chap. 7, 203–45.

> by which the novice accepts apprenticeship to a community which cultivates this lore, appreciates its values and strives to act by its standards. This affiliation begins with the fact that a child submits to education within a community, and is confirmed throughout life to the extent to which the adult continues to place exceptional confidence in the intellectual leaders of the same community.[24]

In the final view, it is a cultural apprenticeship within the believing and worshiping community of Christians that is more important than the cultural apprenticeship in the secular community. The latter, if not vitally informed by the first, will simply shift its fiduciary allegiance to the canons of secular scientism. The university then becomes surrogate church. That is what has happened within the guild of biblical scholarship wherever secular conviviality has become a substitute for the community of Christian belief. Hence biblical scholars need to rediscover the "heuristic intimations" of the believing and worshiping Christian community within its faithful churches, colleges, and theological seminaries, where apprenticeship goes on in obedience to the original call to discipleship. This plea follows Polanyi's observation that we must continually endorse the existing consensus or dissent from it; in so doing we affirm a fiduciary commitment to what we think the true consensus ought to be.[25]

Polanyi observes that the "primitive sentiments of fellowship" that are prior to formal articulation are the basis of shared experience and of joint activities. The fellowship that underlies genuine biblical interpretation cannot therefore be limited to the academic office, classroom, or professional society, but must include at its center the worshiping body of believers who are faithful to the patterns of tradition. Polanyi's observation would apply directly to the need of biblical scholars to be true believers within a believing community: "By fully participating in a ritual, the members of a group affirm the community of their existence, and at the same time identify the life of their group

---

[24]Ibid., 207. His emphasis.

[25]Ibid., 209.

with that of antecedent groups, from whom the ritual has descended to them."[26]

Polanyi describes four coefficients of societal organization that are necessary to form a stable institution,[27] and each is directly applicable to the subject of conviviality. Affirmation and indwelling are articulated as, respectively, the *sharing of convictions*; and the *sharing of a fellowship*; to these is added a third coefficient of *cooperation*, and a fourth, the *exercise of authority or coercion*. Of the modern institutions that embrace the four, universities and churches are the most prominent; but for the biblical interpreter the university or college cannot become a substitute for the believing community from which the Scriptures arose and in which they have been preserved and transmitted. The allegiance of the Christian scholar is first and foremost to the lordship of Christ and his faithful body, and secondarily to the university or college; otherwise one will find in the final analysis that allegiance is only to the university and its secular norms of interpretation, which preempt the fiduciary trust the church has traditionally placed in the Word of God.

The interpreter needs to see that the secular university does not provide an objective perspective on the biblical data, although it claims to be neutrally objectivist. That has been the mistake of post-Enlightenment criticism, and it has culminated in the present crisis in biblical studies. It is Polanyi's point that no opinions, no matter how scientific and objective they are claimed to be, are outside a believing community. The secular university is no exception. The principal difference between the conviviality of the believing Christian community and the conviviality of the secular community is that the latter is functionally nontheistic in its approach to the religious data of Scripture. Walter Wink illustrates the dilemma of the biblical scholar who assumes the tacit commitments of the secular university community. Alluding to Morton Smith and his admission that biblical criticism does not allow for uncontrolla-

[26]Ibid., 211.
[27]Ibid., 212.

ble divine interventions in history (thus excluding the supernatural from the historical method), Wink observes:

> Few practicing biblical scholars would take exception to this, even those who speak of God's acts in history, since these are generally viewed as mediated through the selfhood of human agents. So acclimated are we to this attitude of functional, methodological atheism that we may no longer be shocked by the vast gulf between this view and the Bible's, where God is depicted as directly intervening in nature and history at will! From the outset, therefore, the biblical scholar is committed to a secularist perspective. If he wishes to discover meaning in the texts at all, he has but three choices: he may attempt to interpret the text by a program of demythologization; he may opt for a practicing atheism, whereby references to God in the text are in every case reducible to another explanation; or he may delude himself into believing that there is no hermeneutical problem.[28]

Wink overlooks a fourth choice, which is to accept what Christians have always believed (until very modern times) about the reality of God's supernatural acts in history and to affirm the authoritative witness of the Scriptures to these workings of God on behalf of a fallen race. This is where the hermeneutical line is finally drawn. Although he correctly surmises that historical biblical criticism is bankrupt, Wink is unwilling to return to the conviviality of historic Christianity, but reverts to the sentiments of an older liberalism and a psychologically oriented form of communal exegesis that functions at the pole of religious subjectivity.

The believing community that has not lost its nerve in regard to the authority of Scripture affords the best milieu for arriving at the real meaning and significance of the redemptive acts of biblical history. While its quest for truth is described by certain tacit beliefs—such as the reality of God and his supernatural working in history and nature, the inspiration of Scripture, the deity of Christ, and his substitutionary atonement—these beliefs imply a deep respect for scriptural revela-

[28]Walter Wink, *The Bible in Human Transformation: Toward a New Paradigm for Biblical Study* (Philadelphia: Fortress, 1973), 38–9.

tion and form the parameters within which the Old and New Testaments can once again say what they were intended to say. Contact is made between the Christian interpreter and the evangelists and with Jesus, who is the genesis of the gospel accounts. The evangelical believer shares a common faith with the evangelists of the first century and has confidence in their divinely appointed authority to report correctly who Jesus was, what he said and did, and what his significance was and is. Hence there is a free and open reformist dynamism within the framework of evangelical belief that is like the reformist dynamism of the sixteenth-century Reformers. Functionally atheistic criticism is in fact not free to interpret Jesus and the Gospels (or any of Scripture) authentically because it is motivated by the tacit assumptions of a closed and anthropocentric universe. Such criticism is methodologically incapable of being truly descriptive of the phenomena of Scripture and their ultimate meaning.

Ostensibly free, Polanyi notes, the conviviality of the secular community contains a "menacing contradiction," which those of us who work in the area of biblical studies detect in secular criticism of the Scriptures:

> The great movement of independent thought instilled in the modern mind a desperate refusal of all knowledge that is not absolutely impersonal, and this implied in its turn a mechanical conception of man which was bound to deny man's capacity for independent thought. . . . For when open profession of the great moral passions animating free society are discredited as specious or utopian, its dynamism will tend to be transformed into the hidden driving force of a political machine, which is then proclaimed as inherently right and granted absolute dominion over thought.[29]

Polanyi, whose personal experience spanned the European horrors of Marxist and fascist totalitarianism, unmasks the false ideal of the critical mind in a telling description of how doctrines of behavioral causality have undercut the morality of the Christian tradition and have ended in political and social

[29]Polanyi, *Personal Knowledge*, 214.

bankruptcy. He underscores the fact that there is always a core of personal authority, a conviviality of some sort in every system of thought. But which shall it be: radically liberal or conservative? Speaking of the social malaise of our time, Polanyi asks,

> Can the beliefs of liberalism, no longer believed to be self-evident, be upheld henceforth in the form of an orthodoxy? Can we face the fact that, no matter how liberal a free society may be, it is also profoundly conservative?[30]

The political lessons of the twentieth century with its totalitarian powers bent on radical reforms, ostensibly in pursuit of justice and brotherhood, impressed Polanyi with the fact that the right of moral self-determination and religious freedom can be preserved only within the conviviality of the conservative free society. The truth may be unpalatable to our consciences, he writes, but there is no other way to preserve the free society than to correct unjust privileges within by carefully graded stages, realizing that our duty lies in the service of ideals that we cannot possibly achieve. This also holds true, we may add, in the interpretation of Scripture, the authority of which must be held with conservative allegiance within the confessing community. In gospel criticism, attempts to reinterpret the evangelists' claims under the influence of hostile hermeneutical methods have consistently failed.

The conservative commitment to a creative tradition now brings Polanyi to a powerful articulation of his postcritical hermeneutical philosophy: the justification of personal knowledge in "The Logic of Affirmation," "The Critique of Doubt," and "Commitment." These chapters (8, 9, 10), contain some of the finest hermeneutical thought of modern times and encourage a fresh approach to the inspiration and authority of Scripture and its interpretation. In chapter 8, "The Logic of Affirmation," Polanyi opens his exposition by reviewing succinctly his appraisal of the epistemological situation: we know much more than we can tell, but we know much less than

[30]Ibid., 244.

we previously had thought we could know through the exercise of freedom. He now focuses on the narrow range of knowledge that forms the hard core of greatest certainty.[31] The formal point that is central to his hermeneutical method, and to that of Wittgenstein and I. T. Ramsey, is that we can escape the problem of indefinite regress when we realize that only a speaker or listener can mean something by a word, and that a word in itself means nothing, for it is persons who stand behind words and meaning with personal commitment. Therefore all knowledge is personal knowledge (hence the title of the book, *Personal Knowledge*).

Applied to Jesus' language in the Gospels, this means that the words he speaks mean nothing in themselves, since it is only Jesus as "I am" and "I say to you" who means something *by them*. His words do not have an open texture in and of themselves but convey meaning only through *his* sense of fitness and our confident responsiveness to his sense of fitness.[32] Precise positivistic rules for determining the "authentic" words of Jesus are bound to fail because Jesus personally asserts the factual truth of his statements with "heuristic or persuasive feeling," and understanding comes only from implicit belief both in his authority to speak in this manner and in the personal commitment of the evangelists to report his speech-acts accurately.

> Any attempt to eliminate this personal coefficient, by laying down precise rules for making or testing assertions of fact, is condemned to futility from the start. For we can derive rules of observation and verification only from examples of factual statements that we have accepted as true *before* we knew the rules; and *in the end* the application of our rules will necessarily fall back once more on factual observations, the acceptance of which is an act of personal judgment, unguided by any explicit rules.[33]

---

[31]Ibid., 249.
[32]Ibid., 252–53.
[33]Ibid., 254. His emphasis.

The history of modern biblical criticism has proven this to be the case. In succeeding generations the cultural presuppositions of an era predispose the critic to enter the hermeneutical circle at the point of his tacit critical commitments and in sympathy to what is philosophically in vogue at the time. Two presuppositions that are beyond any possibility of testing, yet have been assumed by every radical critical school, are the doctrines of the closed universe and the autonomy of the critic to interpret the past in terms of the secular present. When these Enlightenment presuppositions are exposed as judgments that are based more on personal preference than on factual evidence, the way is open to offer a hermeneutical approach to the interpretation of Scripture that is more sympathetic to the biblical phenomena themselves. As Polanyi has earlier pointed out, the situation is akin to Gödel's discovery that in mathematics axioms are never self-demonstrable but continually refer to some wider system that always remains richer and ultimately undemonstrable. On the horizon of every form of knowledge one moves toward discovery by shifting from intuition to computation, and from computation to intuition: "The act of assent proves once more to be logically akin to the act of discovery: they are both essentially unformalizable, intuitive mental decisions."[34]

Hence many of the criteria of radical biblical criticism (e.g., dissimilarity, coherence, multiple attestation in gospel criticism) are in themselves insufficient to tell us anything we do not already know, depending on our intuitive presuppositions in regard to the nature of God and of Scripture. If we come to the Gospels in an attitude of faith that is attentive and obedient, the force of Jesus' "I" will address us through the mediating words of the evangelists. If, however, one disclaims Jesus' supernatural claims and those of the early church because of prior allegiance to the biases of secular criticism, he or she will hear only as much as will comfortably fit within that hermeneutical circle. But the latter will lack integrity, since it is unwilling

[34]Ibid., 261.

to bracket those presuppositions that prejudice an openness to the intrinsic validity of the biblical data.

Polanyi attacks the prejudice of scientism as a commitment that is now burned out. The incandescence of the past four or five centuries has combusted on the fuel of the Christian heritage and Greek rationalism. Now we need to go back to our sources:

> Modern man is unprecedented; yet we must now go back to St. Augustine to restore the balance of our cognitive powers. In the fourth century A.D. St. Augustine brought the history of Greek philosophy to a close by inaugurating for the first time a postcritical philosophy. He taught that all knowledge was a gift of grace, for which we must strive under the guidance of antecedent belief: *nisi credideritis, non intelligitis.*[35]

With John Locke and his successors faith was separated from knowledge, and observation and reason became the sole determiners of factual truth. But now that empiricism and rationalism have not offered certitude, Polanyi calls for a return to belief and the fiduciary mode that all along has been functioning surreptitiously in this age of unbelief:

> We must now recognize belief once more as the source of all knowledge. Tacit assent and intellectual passions, the sharing of an idiom and of a cultural heritage, affiliation to a like-minded community: such are the impulses which shape our vision of the nature of things on which we rely for our mastery of things. No intelligence, however critical or original, can operate outside a fiduciary framework.[36]

Hence we must seek liberation from the enervating and bankrupt objectivism of our day, voicing our ultimate convictions from within our convictions, realizing that these are logically prior to any particular assertion of "fact." All knowledge is at root *personal* knowledge, asserted by the "I" who intends the world in this way and who stands behind his words with the commitment of belief. We should freely confess

[35]Ibid., 266. Augustine, *De libero arbitrio*, I.4: "The steps are laid down by the prophet who says, 'Unless ye believe, ye shall not understand.' "

[36]Polanyi, *Personal Knowledge*, 266.

these beliefs that are tacitly taken for granted and accept personal responsibility for them. Knowledge begins not with doubt but with the precritical posture of belief.

This brings Polanyi to the central chapter in his hermeneutical triad, "The Critique of Doubt." The Cartesian mode has deeply influenced the modern age with its call to purge the mind through universal doubt, ridding it of all opinions held in trust. The methodology of doubt goes hand in hand with objectivism, Polanyi avers, and elevates itself into a creed of scientism that is blind and deceptive and leads ultimately to nihilism. All the great discoveries, on the contrary, have been made by believing and intuiting minds in contact with a reality that discloses itself to the indwelling and the obedient. So, in coming to know Jesus in the Gospels we would observe that the authenticity and significance of his language cannot be unlocked by objectivist doubt, which approaches it distantly and impersonally, but only through an attitude of worship and indwelling. Apprehending the sayings and works of Jesus at their deepest level comes only in serving him who speaks and performs them:

> This will lead us back to the conception of religious worship as a heuristic vision and align religion in turn with the great intellectual systems, such as mathematics, fiction and the fine arts, which are validated by becoming happy dwelling places of the human mind.[37]

Unpopular as it may seem to the objectivist critic, there can be no success in focal analysis of the gospel texts until there is first a proper subsidiary trust in the mode of "I believe": "Only a Christian who stands in the service of his faith can understand Christian theology and only he can enter into the religious meaning of the Bible."[38] With that sentence Polanyi presents the case as clearly as it can be made. This approach to the Jesus of the Gospels is radical (i.e., "rooted") in an exactly opposite direction from the radicalism of objectivist criticism. It means that a genuine interpretation of Jesus can be found only from within one's personal commitment to Jesus' personal

[37]Ibid., 280.

[38]Ibid., 281.

claims about himself. No profound truths about him can be discovered through the objectivist method of radical doubt.

While Polanyi betrays some of his own theologically liberal biases in the course of the discussion and makes too much of the difference between theological statements and factual assertions,[39] he nonetheless is persuasive when he describes the circularity of a conceptual system and the way it reinforces itself in contact with fresh topics: it is a kind of "magical framework," a "spell" that provides certain stability.[40] Hence it is inconceivable that any program of comprehensive doubt could succeed. What makes the "when in doubt, discard" hermeneutics of radical gospel criticism dangerous and deceptive is that the advocacy of rational doubt is simply skepticism's way of advocating its own beliefs.

Polanyi sums up the case for his fiduciary hermeneutical method in an important chapter appropriately entitled "Commitment." The leading axiom of his thesis should be underscored: "Any inquiry into our ultimate beliefs can be consistent only if it presupposes its own conclusions. It must be intentionally circular."[41] The logic of any argument, says Polanyi, is but an elaboration of this circle, a systematic course in teaching oneself to hold one's own beliefs. If this sounds subjective, we must remember that it is undertaken within a community where one is held to be personally responsible for his beliefs. That the basic axiom is true, Polanyi has no doubts; the personal participation of the knower in his knowledge is held within a flow of passion and intellectual beauty. Hence, we may remark of the personal conviction and flow of passion with which Jesus is portrayed in the Gospels, as he confidently intends what he says and does to be universally valid, and in light of which life-or-death responses must be made.

The dilemma of the radical objectivist critic is that he is "caught in an insoluble conflict between a demand for an

[39]Ibid., 282–84. His affinity for Paul Tillich's two domains is especially weak and reflects a lingering Kantian dualism.

[40]Ibid., 289–90.

[41]Ibid., 299. Again note the similarity of this presuppositional approach to that of Van Til.

impersonality which would discredit all commitment and an urge to make up his mind which drives him to recommit himself."[42] What the radical objectivist often does, if he is a biblical critic and claims some commitment to Christian faith, is to play two language-games at once: one with the secular circle where the credo of conviviality is radical skepticism (even atheism), and the other with a worshiping community where the credo of conviviality is religious belief. But how can the two worlds be brought together in such an illogical dualism?

> The answer is this. The "actual facts" are accredited facts, as seen within the commitment situation, while subjective beliefs are the conviction accrediting these facts as seen noncommittally by someone not sharing them.[43]

That is to say, for example, that while the authenticity of the sayings of Jesus in the Gospels may be arrived at by a number of different methods of analysis, at base a skeptical objectivism that dismisses the supernatural will inevitably end up with a shorter list and a Jesus quite different from that of the evangelists and historical orthodoxy. In that case Jesus will not be allowed to make any explicit claims that he considers himself Messiah and God incarnate. The objectivist-naturalist approach is self-defeating, however, because on its own grounds it must admit that the core sayings of Jesus bear witness to claims that are implicitly christological and messianic.[44] Thus an open fiduciary approach to the Gospels (i.e., recognizing that they authentically represent the intention of Jesus by way of faithful eye-witnesses) is more stable simply because it fulfills the requirements of the criterion of coherence. Since Jesus makes implicit messianic claims, it is in character for him to make explicit messianic claims as well. There is, accordingly, no impersonal objective criterion by which to distinguish the early

---

[42]Ibid., 304.

[43]Ibid.

[44]See Royce Gordon Gruenler, *New Approaches to Jesus and the Gospels* (Grand Rapids: Baker, 1982), chapters 1–5, for application, interpretation, and critique of the criteria of radical criticism.

church's Christology from the claims of Jesus himself. Jesus emerges as the origin or genesis of the tradition.[45]

The descriptive (or phenomenological) method we have been using affirms the stability and coherence of the gospel tradition because Jesus is seen to indwell its truth-claims that the new age of salvation has been inaugurated and that he is, in his own creative way, the Christ, the promised Messiah, the incarnate Son of God, and Son of Man. This classically orthodox affirmation of the Gospels' empirical truth-claims rests on the authority of Jesus' "I say," "I am," and "look and see" speech-acts. Of such empirical truth-claims Polanyi writes,

> An empirical statement is true to the extent to which it reveals an aspect of reality, a reality largely hidden to us, and *existing therefore independently of our knowing it*. . . . The inquiring scientist's intimations of a hidden reality are personal. They are his own beliefs, which—owing to his originality—as yet he alone holds. Yet they are not a subjective state of mind, but convictions held with universal intent, and heavy with arduous projects. . . . In a heuristic commitment, affirmation, surrender and legislation are fused into a single thought, bearing on a hidden reality.[46]

This describes our project and our commitment as we reaffirm the convictions of the historic Christian community in a contemporary evangelical setting, finding there a "happy dwelling place" of the mind and heart. There the reality of God speaks with more stability and coherence through the empirical disclosure of the authoritative and redeeming Jesus who generates an authentic tradition. This is the orthodox Christian's intellectual commitment for which he or she accepts

[45]For an example of a new literary approach to the Gospels that is neo-Gnostic and assigns Jesus' central Christological claims to the theological-literary creation of the evangelist and his church setting, see Frank Kermode, *The Genesis of Secrecy* (Cambridge: Harvard University Press, 1979); for an adaptation of the method, see R. A. Culpepper, *Anatomy of the Fourth Gospel* (Philadelphia: Fortress, 1983).

[46]Polanyi, *Personal Knowledge*, 311. His emphasis.

personal responsibility: "*This acceptance is the sense of my calling.*"[47]

What then of the "hard" questions, e.g., the variations in historical detail among the Gospels? In answer, one must look first at the overall evidence and the larger picture of personal commitment, stability, and coherence of the evangelists' reportage (and Jesus' promise to authenticate their witness, [John 14:26; 15:26]) before dealing with smaller difficulties inductively. That is the way all practicing scientists function in their areas of research. One of the most widely held theories in secular Western culture is the naturalistic evolution of the species, yet there are many inductive problems in the theory with which the believing scientist makes peace, simply because it offers an ordered picture, given a prior personal commitment to naturalism. Polanyi observes that "neo-Darwinism is firmly accredited and highly regarded by science, though there is little evidence for it, because it beautifully fits into a mechanistic system of the universe and bears on a subject—the origin of man—which is of the utmost intrinsic interest."[48]

If the practicing natural scientist is dependent on personal commitments to theories that contain evidential problems, the practicing Christian cannot be faulted for making personal commitments to a view that he believes brings the greatest coherence and stability to human existence and best explains the data surrounding Jesus: belief in the divine inspiration of Scripture. The fiduciary commitments of competing systems must be addressed first: Is the interpreter open or closed to the world of the Bible; does he claim autonomy over its texts and the claims of its authoritative figures, in particular the incarnate Son of God; or is he willing to be attentive to what they say and to humble himself in believing acceptance of God's self-disclosure? The results of any inductive analysis of the biblical texts will be determined by one's answers to this fundamental question.

In retrospect of the past several generations, biblical

[47]Ibid., 322. His emphasis.
[48]Ibid., 136.

criticism has cause to be embarrassed by its meager results and its often negative effect on the role of the Bible in the church when it has reflected the biases of the times. On the other hand, where biblical scholarship has undertaken its task in obedience to God's Word, rather than in a supposed neutral objectivism, powerful results have been brought about in the life of the church and in its mission. Once this "postcritical," postnaturalistic hermeneutical method is adopted, the major variations among historical accounts in Scripture (e.g., Kings/Chronicles in the Old Testament and the Gospels in the New Testament) may be resolved by the criteria of complementary aspection and paraphrastic freedom with which the biblical writers are inspired to present and adapt the events of redemptive history for their readers. The authors of Scripture know more than they can tell, and it is not the interpreter's calling (or capability) to impugn their testimony and assume a superior position of critical neutrality. In Polanyi's view that all knowledge is personal knowledge accredited by one's affirmation of a particular worldview, it would not be surprising if some problems remain unresolved, for we know more than we can tell and can tell in purely abstract scientific terms far less than we once thought.

Accordingly, a truly postcritical hermeneutical philosophy will not concern itself primarily with the minutiae of analytical questions, though these will be a secondary focus of interest, but with the larger issue of how the interpreter reads the biblical texts—whether in doubt as a disbeliever who undertakes to uncover a conspiracy of sorts in the historical accounts of Scripture, or in commitment as a believer in the ability of the biblical historians to convey the real meaning of history from God's point of view. Once that initial posture is decided on (Polanyi reminds us that both are fiduciary), the analytical details of the texts can be addressed. There may be unresolvable problems facing the interpreter at points, but as Polanyi says, "A fiduciary philosophy does not eliminate doubt, but (like Christianity) says that we should hold on to what we truly believe. . . , trusting the unfathomable intimations that call upon us to do so."[49]

In accepting with gratitude the truth-claims of the biblical authors' interpretation of the real world, believers attest their sense of calling and response to God's self-disclosure. In the affirmation of personal convictions held with universal intent, we perform our spiritual and scholarly obligations by openly committing ourselves in belief to the integrity of the biblical witnesses who have bequeathed to us the inestimable gift of God's redeeming revelation.

---

[49]Ibid., 318.

FOR FURTHER READING

A complete list of works cited may be found in the index of modern authors and titles. In this section I have selected contributions in English that should prove especially helpful as introductions to the major topics covered in this book.

Familiarity with original philosophical sources is important for further study. The reader may approach this somewhat daunting task in two ways: first, by pursuing selected materials in edited and annotated anthologies, such as those by Walter Kaufmann, and Barrett and Aiken (see index); second, by reading the works of selected authors in inexpensive paperback editions. Consult *Books in Print* under author or title in the nearest library for most recent and available editions, with prices. Selections from Kant, Schleiermacher, Hegel, and Kierkegaard are of special interest, since their works have had greater influence on philosophical and hermeneutical thought in the nineteenth and twentieth centuries.

Historical studies from an evangelical perspective that give an overview and interpretation of the history and problems of Western philosophy in the compass of a single volume:

Colin Brown, *Christianity & Western Thought: A History of Philosophic Ideas and Movements*, vol. 1 (Downers Grove, IL: InterVarsity, 1990).

__________, *History and Faith: A Personal Exploration* (Grand Rapids: Academie Books, Zondervan, 1989).

Edward John Carnell, *An Introduction to Christian Apologetics: A Philosophic Defense of the Trinitarian-Theistic Faith* (Grand Rapids: Eerdmans, 1948). Although not a history of philosophy per se, this book underscores the importance of the problem of the one and the many throughout classical philosophy to the present, and was one of the first Christian studies to awaken my interest in philosophy.

Gordon H. Clark, *Thales to Dewey: A History of Philosophy* (Boston: Houghton Mifflin, 1957).

Frederick J. Copleston, *A History of Philosophy*, Book Two, Descartes to Kant; Book Three, Fichte to Sartre (New York: Doubleday, 1986).

Norman L. Geisler and Winfried Corduan, *Philosophy of Religion*, 2d ed. (Grand Rapids: Baker, 1988).

Interpretive hermeneutical studies of special significance for the evangelical:

D. A. Carson and John D. Woodbridge, eds., *Hermeneutics, Authority, and Canon* (Grand Rapids: Academie Books, Zondervan, 1986).

Kelly Clark, *Return to Reason: A Critique of Enlightenment Evidentialism and a Defense of Reason and Belief in God* (Grand Rapids: Eerdmans, 1990).

Ronald Feenstra and Cornelius Plantinga, Jr., eds., *Trinity, Incarnation, and Atonement* (South Bend: University of Notre Dame, 1989). Essays by philosophers and theologians on some of the most difficult traditional issues.

John Frame, *The Doctrine of the Knowledge of God* (Phillipsburg, N.J.: Presbyterian and Reformed, 1987).

Royce Gordon Gruenler, *The Inexhaustible God: Biblical Faith and the Challenge of Process Theism* (Grand Rapids: Baker, 1983).

Paul Helm, *The Divine Revelation: The Basic Issues* (Westchester, IL: Crossway, 1982).

Carl F. H. Henry, *God, Revelation and Authority: God Who Speaks and Shows*, vol. 4 (Waco: Word, 1979).

Dallas M. High, *Language, Persons and Belief: Studies in Wittgenstein's Philosophical Investigations, and Religious Uses of Language* (New York: Oxford University, 1967).

Arthur F. Holmes, *Christian Philosophy in the Twentieth Century: An Essay in Philosophical Methodology* (Nutley, N.J.: Craig, 1969).

————, *Contours of a World View* (Grand Rapids: Eerdmans, 1983).

————, *The Making of a Christian Mind: A Christian World View and the Academic Enterprise* (Downers Grove, IL: InterVarsity, 1985).

Thomas S. Kuhn, *The Structure of Scientific Revolutions*, 2d ed. (Chicago: University of Chicago, 1970).

Wolfhart Pannenberg, *Metaphysics and the Idea of God* (Grand Rapids: Eerdmans, 1990).

Alvin Plantinga and Nicholas Wolterstorff, *Faith and Rationality: Reason and Belief in God* (South Bend: University of Notre Dame, 1983).

Michael Polanyi, *Personal Knowledge: Towards a Post-Critical Philosophy* (New York: Harper & Row, 1964).

Vern Poythress, *Science and Hermeneutics* (Grand Rapids: Academie Books, Zondervan, 1988).

Earl D. Radmacher and Robert D. Preus, eds., *Hermeneutics, Inerrancy, and the Bible* (Grand Rapids: Academie Books, Zondervan, 1984).

Ian T. Ramsey, *Religious Language: An Empirical Placing of Theological Phrases* (London: SCM, 1957).

Paul A. Schilpp and Lewis E. Hahn, eds., *Gabriel Marcel* (LaSalle, IL: Open Court, 1984).

Anthony C. Thiselton, *The Two Horizons: New Testament Hermeneutics and Philosophical Description* (Grand Rapids: Eerdmans, 1984).

Cornelius Van Til, *The Defense of the Faith* (Philadelphia: Presbyterian and Reformed, 1955).

________, *The New Hermeneutic* (Nutley, N.J.: Presbyterian and Reformed, 1974.

Nicholas Wolterstorff, *Reason Within the Bounds of Religion*, 2d ed. (Grand Rapids: Eerdmans, 1984).

Studies that reflect the remodelling of classical theology through modern liberal hermeneutics critiqued in this book:

Rudolf Bultmann, *Jesus Christ and Mythology* (London: SCM, 1960).

Sarah Coakley, *Christ Without Absolutes: A Study of the Christology of Ernst Troeltsch* (New York: Oxford University, 1989).

Peter C. Hodgson and Robert H. King, eds., *Christian Theology: An Introduction to Its Traditions and Tasks* (Philadelphia: Fortress, 1985). Deconstructs classical theology and reconstructs according to modern philosophical hermeneutics.

Peter C. Hodgson, *God in History: Shapes of Freedom* (Nashville: Abingdon, 1989). Employs Troeltsch and Hegel as a framework for hermeneutics and argues for the correlative realities of God and history.

Sallie McFague, *Models of God: Theology for an Ecological, Nuclear Age* (Philadelphia: Fortress, 1987). Argues that all language about God is metaphorical (God is mother, lover, friend) but makes no propositional truth claims.

Edgar McKnight, *Postmodern Use of the Bible: The Emergence of Reader-Oriented Criticism* (Nashville: Abingdon, 1988). Analyzes contemporary hermeneutical alternatives.

Schubert Ogden, *Faith and Freedom: Toward a Theology of Liberation* (Nashville: Abingdon, 1989). Utilizes the hermeneutics of process theism and liberation theology.

Recommended for ongoing hermeneutical interaction from a Christian philosophical perspective:

Faith and Philosophy: Journal of the Society of Christian Philosophers (Asbury College, Wilmore KY 40390-1198).

INDEX OF AUTHORS/TITLES

INDEX OF SUBJECTS

INDEX OF BIBLICAL PASSAGES